HOW TO SELL ART

A Systematic Approach to Creating Relationships
with Collectors and Closing the Sale

A Guide for Artists and Gallerists

J. Jason Horejs

RedDot Press | Phoenix, AZ

To Carrie

Special thanks to Karly Williams for her tireless efforts in editing the book

Table of Contents

INTRODUCTION

Several years ago, I happened to be in the gallery alone when a couple walked through the front door. I left my desk to greet and welcome them to the gallery. Both the husband and wife responded to my greeting with beautiful British accents, and I learned that they were visiting Arizona from England. I had the sense that they were a bit hurried. They explained that their time was limited and they hoped to visit as many galleries as possible during their stay. After offering my services to assist them in any way I could, I stepped back to allow them to look around the gallery.

I don't remember exactly what was going through my mind as the couple toured the gallery, but I'm certain I had no expectations of making a sale. Through years of experience, I have found that the more time I can keep potential buyers in the gallery, the more likely I am to close a sale. These two, however, were moving through the gallery at a clipped pace that would have them out the door in a flash.

They traversed the gallery in a clockwise pattern, which put them on a path toward the gallery entrance. When they paused in front of a large sculpture of Albert Einstein sitting on a park bench, I observed the wife whispering in her husband's ear; but before I could approach them to talk about the piece, they moved on. As they began their exit, I followed them to the door and thanked them for their visit, whereupon the husband turned to me and pulled a business card from his wallet.

"We're interested in the Einstein for our garden," he said. "Can you email me some information about the piece?"

"Of course," I replied. "I'll shoot you the information with an image of the piece right away."

"Wonderful," the gentleman said, "thank you very much."

With that they were gone. The couple couldn't have spent more than three or four minutes in the gallery. While I was obviously excited about the prospect of having interest in a major piece such as the Einstein figure, experience again led me to remain skeptical about the chance of successfully closing the sale. I have found that once a client has left the building, the odds of making a sale decline dramatically. The clients may have truly liked the idea of the piece, but time and distance have a way of diminishing interest.

I sat down immediately after they left, and sent an email with the information about the size and price of the piece, along with a few images. I included a courteous note thanking them for their visit. I then added the couple to my follow up list and went on with my day.

Over the course of the next few weeks, I sent several emails and left a message at the husband's office to determine whether they remained interested. With each attempted contact, my confidence in the possibility of successfully closing the sale waned.

One can only imagine my surprise, then, when I received the following email:

Hello Jason,

Thanks, and yes we want to buy.

My plan is to send you an e-mail on Sunday to follow-up.

I have been extraordinarily busy at work since we returned to the UK, so sorry for not responding earlier.

You could have knocked me over with a feather. I received the promised email that Sunday, asking for wire transfer instructions and giving me delivery information. The wire transfer was completed within the next week. I called my shipping company and made arrangements for them to pick up the piece, and it was then on its way to England.

From start to finish, I could not have spent more than a couple of hours putting the sale together. However, this process does not always work so smoothly, as can be illustrated with another experience I had several years earlier.

One evening, just after the dinner hour, we were getting ready to close when a gentleman walked through the door into the gallery. I introduced myself and we started a conversation. The gentleman (whom I will call "Ed") was a successful local business owner, and was delightfully personable. We chatted about his business, and about a home he was in the process of remodeling. I showed him around the gallery and told him about various artists we represented.

We paused before the work of a particular artist; Ed was clearly captivated by the style, as well as the subject matter. I proceeded to tell him about the artist's background and inspiration.

His work was infused with all the wonder, passion, and splendor of his travels through the Southwest and into Northern Mexico. Ed was especially interested in learning about what animated these paintings, because he and his wife were remodeling their home with heavy Mexican Colonial influences.

Ed further contemplated the work and decided that it would fit perfectly into his home. When he said he would show images of the work to his wife if I would email them to him, I took Ed's contact information and immediately sent images of all the pieces of interest.

Though I didn't know it at the time, that first meeting with Ed marked the beginning of a transaction of epoch duration: it required many long months of protracted effort to close the sale. After sending the first email and getting no response, I followed up with my usual battery of emails, notes, and phone calls. I was surprised by how long it took to actually get Ed and his wife back into the gallery after his initial visit; he had seemed so impressed by the art, and anxious to share his discovery with his spouse.

When they finally did come in six weeks after our initial meeting, Ed's wife (whom I will call "Liz") also liked the work, albeit not the same pieces preferred by her husband. We discussed their home and the spaces that needed artwork, and approximated the number and sizes of pieces required to fit the spaces. I asked Ed and Liz to mutually decide upon the subject matter that would best support their décor.

While we conversed, I made detailed notes. We determined that we might be able to use some work already available in the gallery, but that we would likely need to commission the artist to create additional site-specific work. We ultimately decided that it would make sense for me to visit the home with the artist and have a look at the space.

There was only one problem to deter us in the immediate execution of our plan: the home was in the midst of a major phase of the remodel, and many of the spaces we would be working to fill didn't yet exist. We all agreed to keep in touch and get back together when this particular phase of the remodel was completed. Ed felt confident that we would be able to reconvene in four months' time.

Four months stretched into six. During those six months, I made sure I stayed in touch with the clients so they wouldn't have a chance to forget about the art. I also had several conversations with the artist, telling him about the clients and their interests. In the course of his normal work, he created pieces that we agreed would likely meet the clients' needs.

When I finally received word that Ed and Liz's home was far enough along for us to see the space, I went right away to take measurements. Ed showed me around the house and explained with pride how they were creating their perfect haven.

Rather than simply have the architect design their home from scratch and mimic the Mexican style they were trying to achieve, Ed and Liz asked him to include architectural elements they had found during their extensive travels through Sonora and Guadalajara. Many of the doors were from old Spanish pueblos. A number of important furniture pieces were picked up in shops and trucked to Arizona. The tiles for the roof were hand crafted by Mexican artisans who used a traditional technique that shaped the tiles individually by molding them to their thighs.

As the house tour continued, Ed explained that the floor tiles were also hand crafted. He regaled me with the story of his finding an old soda vending machine, and showed me where he had placed it, near the swimming pool. The effects of their efforts were spectacular, and it was easy to see that Ed and Liz were very proud of their home.

After an hour's walk-about, I started taking measurements of the art spaces, and recording them in my notebook. I also took hundreds of photos to clearly depict and define the spaces.

When I got back to the gallery, I put together a dossier with all of the information, and had it delivered to the artist. He studied the contents of the dossier, and contacted me to say he was ready to scout the inventory for art that might serve our purposes.

It took the two of us a week to select and gather the paintings we felt were right. With this task accomplished, we called Ed and Liz to schedule an appointment to show them the work. By now, however, Liz was traveling for several weeks, and upon her return she and Ed would both be taking a two-week trip to Europe. Thus, another delay.

It was a month before we all got our schedules synchronized and were able to meet. The artist and I drove a van filled with art to the house and started parading it in. We tried pieces in different spaces, and quickly determined that at least two were going to be perfect fits. Others were the right composition and color, but the wrong size. By the time we finished that day, we knew that two of the pieces we brought were fine for installation, but that two more pieces needed to be commissioned.

The house was still six weeks from completion, giving us a little time to work. However, the clients had scheduled a house-warming party to take place shortly after their home was finished, making it critical that the artwork be ready in time for the celebration.

We finally had a package put together, and could proceed with negotiations. Ed hadn't become a successful businessman by accident: the man could negotiate! We went round and round on pricing. We gave him a number calculated to include a collector's discount, whereupon he gave us a number he felt was "more reasonable". We countered and suggested minor modifications to the sizes of the pieces, to better fit the budget he had in mind.

After several days of phone calls and emails, we finally reached a consensus. Ed gave us a deposit that enabled the artist to get started on the commissioned pieces. We held the others at the gallery.

Finally, a month later, the pieces were finished and the house was far enough along for us to deliver and install the artwork. The artist and I took the four pieces to the house, and together with Ed and Liz, hung the artwork in the home. The atmosphere was festive, and Ed and Liz expressed how pleased they were with the art. They enthused that the paintings were the finishing touch to their incredible remodeling project.

Though I didn't keep an exact reckoning of all of the time I spent in putting the sale together, I am certain I spent 80-100 hours working out all of the details, and interacting with the clients. There were some tense moments along the way, especially during negotiations, when it seemed the sale would never come together, which just made it all the sweeter when it did.

Two diverse scenarios, two diverse sales. One could easily wish that every sale was like the sale of the Einstein bench: more a matter of being in the right place, at the right time, with the right piece of artwork, than that of any skill on my part. While I certainly love making the "easy" sale, I have a confession to make: I enjoy the hard one as well.

A great sense of satisfaction comes from knowing one's efforts have made the difference in a customer's decision to buy. Even more satisfying is the knowledge that, thanks to one's skill and exertion, the collector will enjoy the artwork for many years to come.

Many individuals I encounter in the art world, be they artists, gallery personnel, or agents, take a devil-may-care approach to selling art. The assumption is that selling artwork is a soft-sale process, wherein the artwork sells itself. While this may sometimes be the case, why cop the attitude? Frequently, what one says or fails to say will make all the difference. Yes, one will make the easy sale no matter what he does; but his ability to follow through on the hard ones will ultimately determine his success in selling art.

This book is written with two audiences in mind: professional artists, and the professionals who work in and operate galleries. While the technique and advice I share here will smoothly transition from one group to the other, each reader will face unique challenges and opportunities when selling art, regardless of particular circumstances.

Throughout the book, I will write in general terms to both groups. However, my words will often cater more specifically to the professional artist who is trying to market and sell his own work. I trust that gallery professionals will not take offense at this approach. I fully intend the book to be read by both artists and gallery professionals, but must acknowledge that the number of professional artists far exceeds the number of gallerists in the industry. Therefore, I will ask gallerists to forgive me when I frequently reference "your art" or "your work". Know that the counsel also applies to the art salesperson, even if she is not selling her own work.

To the Artist Reading this Book

In my first book, *"Starving" to Successful | The Fine Artist's Guide to Getting into Galleries and Selling More Art,* I sought to give the artist a clear and concise picture of what she would need to do to build a successful relationship with a gallery.

I remain convinced that gallery relationships are vital to one's long-term success, yet must acknowledge that we are living in a new age. Technological tools, including the internet, make it increasingly possible for one to manage her own career, and to connect directly with collectors. The artist not only has to create her best work, but must also organize a business, and become an expert at marketing and selling her work. This book will help you, the artist, to become a crack salesperson.

Even the artist who is already showing in galleries is going to benefit from an improved knowledge of the sales process. Every artist will undoubtedly have the opportunity to interact with buyers at various points throughout her career — my intention in these pages is to assist her (or him) to be prepared to successfully navigate such interactions.

Becoming a great salesperson takes work. WORK. And MORE WORK

How long did it take you to become an expert at creating your art? Though many artists are gifted with incredible talent, and begin to express this talent early in their lives, few people are born great artists. Talent must be cultivated, technique must be nurtured, and experience must be harvested. Becoming a great artist takes time and work; it is a journey; it is an evolution.

Another question to contemplate: Which do you find to be more difficult, creating your art, or selling it? If you are like most artists I know, you won't hesitate in answering this question – while creating art is a pleasure, selling it can be a challenge (to say the least). Just as it takes talent, study, and experience to create great artwork, it takes more than a modicum of effort to become a great salesperson. Creating a sale, just like creating a piece of artwork, is a process comprised of various steps and technical procedures.

To the Gallery Owner or Salesperson Reading this Book

When I set out to write this book, I had a simple plan: to write the book I wish had been available to me in the early 1990's, when I was getting started in the gallery business. I have always been an avid reader, and believe that knowledge is the key to success in any field. Be that as it is, why not share some of the lessons I have learned along the way, and perhaps spare the reader the worst of my mistakes.

I first started working in a gallery when I was seventeen, but didn't get a chance to start selling until I had been employed for about a year. I still remember my first sale, and the excitement I experienced when shaking the clients' hands to close the deal. It may be a huge cliché, but I knew at that moment I wanted to spend my life selling art. From that time forward, I kept close watch on my colleagues in the gallery – observing how they worked, and listening to what they said to clients.

I also began looking for books about selling art. It has been my lifelong inclination to turn to the printed word. At the time, I couldn't find a single book on the topic. While there were hundreds of books on selling in general, nowhere was there to be found a book specifying the "art of selling art".

Selling art is similar to selling other goods in some ways, but it is different in others. I quickly came to realize this when I started reading books by famous salesmen like Zig Ziglar. Though I learned a great deal from these writers, and even recommend reading their books, in this book I want to give advice that ought to be put to direct use in day-to-day encounters with art buyers.

Gallery owners, directors, and salespeople, like artists, wear many different hats. Though much of the work overlaps, it is always helpful to think of each role one plays separately, and to focus on improving in that area. For example, a gallery owner is often a businessperson, a human-resources manager, a marketer, a salesperson. He undoubtedly wears the hats of curator and janitor, when playing these roles, as well. Gallery staff might double as record keeper, personal assistant, salesperson, greeter, or custodian. The possible scenarios for character development are staggering.

Giving due consideration to all of these roles one must play to be in the business, only one role deserves top billing, and that is the role of salesperson. The fact is, no other roles need be cast at all if art is not selling. Yet often these lesser roles, with their lesser tasks, will get in the way of the salesman selling.

How often have I been sitting at the computer fretting over a bit of bookkeeping, an email, or some other trivial task, only to ignore a customer? Even worse have been the occasions when people have walked through the gallery door, and I have resented their intrusions upon my time.

If there were ever a case of misprioritizing, this has to be it. It can be difficult to address the internal conflict that arises when we are faced with a major challenge that requires our full attention, yet must simultaneously manage the lesser issues which threaten to engulf us. The reality is that we are in a business that rarely allows us to put our full energy into sales. Customers must, however, be our first priority, as they are our bread and butter. Blaming them for fragmenting our time with their comings and goings is an exercise in self-defeat.

I suggest you look at your day in a different way. Focus on sales, and consider anything else you have to do to be the distraction. Try to organize your time and compartmentalize your tasks, thus enabling you to concentrate all of your resources upon the victory of the sale. How about doing your bookkeeping early in the morning, before you open the doors for business? Do your inventory and your paperwork when someone else can watch the sales floor and attend to customers.

Do remember you are a *salesperson* and not a *sales clerk*. I have encountered many sales clerks in the gallery business over the years, and some have been quite effective in their passive approach of waiting for a sale to happen. Once a client has decided to buy art, the clerk can prove competent and efficient in completing the mechanical aspects of the sale. In contrast, a salesperson is enthusiastically proactive: she doesn't wait for the sale; she makes it happen. The salesperson looks for opportunities to offer superior service to the gallery's clients, and employs her considerable skills to help them acquire artwork that will enhance their homes and enrich their lives.

What I offer in these pages is a guideline for selling art. This guide is a synthesis of information, knowledge, and experience gleaned from my twenty years of interaction with thousands of customers. As is always true with the school of life, I have learned from my successes as well as my failures. Through it all, I have learned that no two sales are alike. How could it be otherwise, seeing that no two customers are alike: each has unique needs and a distinctive personality.

The techniques and strategies offered in this book are designed to increase your effectiveness in your work with customers to close sales. If all that were required to sell art were the chanting of a few magic words or the bestowing of a magnanimous smile, this book would be superfluous. But because you live in the real world, where real success is won by real work, you had best learn the art of real salesmanship.

Top notch salesmanship demands agility in adapting to the needs and desires of the customer. Understanding the sales process will enable you to become more agile and skilled in guiding each customer toward a sale. A firmness in purpose and a clarity in vision will facilitate the sealing of the deal.

I know I haven't yet begun the book. Nevertheless, I want to go ahead and share what I have found to be the secret to sales success. This is not the sort of secret you learn by making a pilgrimage to visit a guru on the top of a mountain, or a wizard in a distant city - there's nothing "mystical" nor "magical" about it. It's simply this: your goal is not to sell, but rather to help your customer buy. There is a big difference.

You may already know there are few things more gratifying than selling art – whether it's your own, or someone else's. When things are going right, the process is exhilarating, challenging, and fun. The more you know about the process, the more things will go right. So with that, let's dive in.

Chapter 1 | Preparation

The Boy Scouts have a simple but great motto: "Be Prepared." This motto gives impetus to a young scout's extensive training in the mastery of a vast array of skills. A scout works to prepare himself to meet a variety of situations, everything from dealing with medical emergencies to outfitting himself for extended wilderness expeditions. While the motto itself may be simple, the assignment of actually preparing oneself is a complex process, and for a young scout entails years of training and progressive exposure to new challenges.

Anything that is worthwhile is worthy of preparation, and selling art is no exception. Stepping into a selling situation without preparing for it would be like sending a scout to winter camp without a sleeping bag, without training for surviving the cold, and without knowledge of frostbite prevention. If you have ever gone into an art-selling situation without preparation, you know that comparing it to a bone-chilling excursion into the wilderness is more than mere metaphor; you truly will be out in the cold.

Just as in scouting, training to sell art requires both mental and physical preparation. Each time the salesperson has an opportunity to meet potential clients with the goal to sell art, she must be prepared to make use of her entire arsenal of sales tools and strategies. The posture of readiness invites the confidence and trust of the customer.

Put Your Mind in a Selling State

Immediately prior to a gallery opening, an art festival, or any other selling opportunity, take a few minutes to clear your mind and shift into selling mode. Often an artist will spend days physically preparing to install and display his artwork, but fail to take a moment to mentally prepare for the work ahead. A gallerist may spend the day lighting artwork, printing out price tags, and setting out the wine and cheese before an opening, yet not put a thought toward the selling task ahead.

The stressors of the final rush to make ready for a showing will sometimes play havoc with the mental state of an artist or gallerist. In the minutes she meets the first prospective buyer, instead of focusing on serving a collector's needs, and engaging the potential client in a proactive way, the salesperson finds herself simply reacting in an automatic way, or worse yet, not acting at all. Taking on the form of an automaton, she loses her focus and comes across as preoccupied and distracted. Not good. Not good at all.

During the lead-in to any opportunity to sell, take a few moments and a few deep breaths to clear your mind of the entire pre-show hubbub. Be in the moment. Focus solely on the essential task at hand: Selling.

Take five minutes to read a chapter of this book to allow a single principle to penetrate your mind. Commit to focusing on that one principle throughout the hours ahead. Once your mind has shifted into sales mode, throw yourself into the event with enthusiasm and energy – don't let your attention wander. Feel the excitement. Exude joy. You are now in your element!

To The Gallery Owner or Director:

Treat the half-hour prior to a gallery opening as a pre-game: You are the coach and the sales-staff is your team. Go over the strategy for the opening. Reiterate the most important aspects of the art, and review what staff should say about the artist. If possible, have the artist herself share what she feels is the most interesting aspect of the art. Remind everyone that each person who walks through the front door is a potential buyer and should be fully engaged.

Of course, all of this will require preparation on your part ahead of time – I suggest re-reading the artist's bio in the days leading up to a show. Walk through the gallery with the artist and ask her to share her thoughts on each piece of artwork.

This pre-game pep-talk will focus your staff and lead to greater customer service and increased sales.

Assume You are Going to Sell

Past experience may have taught you that you're not always going to be successful at selling your art. We've all had openings that have, despite our best efforts, bombed. Some days the stars simply don't align. While this is frustrating, it can also be dangerous, especially if it happens more than once. Soon you can find yourself in a mindset prior to a show, wherein you simply accept not selling as the norm. It is tempting to let this happen, because once you have, the pressure is off. If you have low expectations, there is no possibility of disappointment, and any sales that come are happy, unexpected surprises.

This danger is even greater for a gallerist in the day-to-day routine of a gallery, in which apathy can quickly take hold. Once you have settled into this way of thinking, your entire attitude and posture follow. Now instead of eagerly greeting each potential buyer, you sit in your chair with the latest novel, glancing up when people approach. "Let me know if you have any questions," you lamely greet them.

A vicious cycle has begun. Your low expectations have lulled you into thinking you need no longer bother. Your sales decrease. Your expectations continue to plummet.

Break the cycle now! At the beginning of each event (or day, for that matter), prepare yourself to give 100% in the sales effort. Proceed with the assumption that you are going to sell, and conduct yourself accordingly.

Dress for Success

I could easily draw analogies between selling art and performing on the stage. Going into a selling situation is much like going onstage: you have to shed your naturally shy, reticent personality, and step into character as a bold, confident, and successful salesperson. Nothing will help you step into this character like dressing for the part.

Suiting up in well-pressed, appropriate clothing will instantly increase your confidence. Of course, you will choose your clothing based upon the context of a particular event. A gallery opening dictates a sport coat, or perhaps a suit and tie for the gentleman, and a dress, or suit and heels for the lady. An outdoor show is going to be less formal — business-casual attire will fit the bill - slacks and a tailored shirt or blouse will work just fine.

An artist has a bit of leeway to introduce some color into his wardrobe. I have encountered artists who can pull off very colorful, gypsy-like getups, where the bohemian clothing and jewelry are themselves works of art. Just be careful not to overdo it – you risk scaring your customers off if they feel you are "too far out there". Never present yourself in a costume that makes you appear to be unapproachable.

Before a major gallery opening, go ahead and splurge: buy a whole new outfit. You want to project an aura of success to your clients, and nothing helps you feel like a million bucks more than dressing in new, stylish clothes.

Always Have Your Tools Ready

The assumption that you are going to sell, along with the clothing that fits the occasion, together with the chapter you have read, have put you in the mental zone for sales success. You now want to turn your attention to the necessary tangibles. It is vital to have everything you need readily available to execute the sale.

Following, find listed the bare-minimum in supplies necessary for a sales transaction. You will further develop this list by adding the items you find useful in selling your work.

- ***Sales Slips***

Always keep a supply of sales slips readily at hand. You can pick up a basic sales slip with carbon copies at any office supply store, or you can order customized slips online to include your logo and contact information.

- ***Business Cards***

While business cards are quickly losing their practical value (how many people maintain a rolodex anymore?), they do make you look more professional when interacting with clients. I'll explain later why having a customer's email address is about a million times more effective than giving out your business card. That being said, I still use business cards.

I suggest putting as much contact information as possible on the card. Include all of your phone numbers, email addresses, and websites. My customers are always impressed when I show them that my mobile number is on the card, and that they can contact me directly anytime the need arises.

Consider including an image of artwork on the back of the card. The artwork adds interest to the card, and will serve as a good reminder to the client of a specific connection to you and to your gallery.

- *Brochures*

Later in the book, in a different context, I will explain why I feel that a brochure should be a tool of last resort. Frankly, I hesitate to give clients brochures; I would rather send them home with a piece of artwork. That being said, there will be times when you will find it advantageous to send an interested client on his way with images of the work, as well as with pertinent contact information.

- *Bubble Wrap / Bags / Boxes*

I once sold a necklace to a client who had fallen in love with the piece's unique design. She was on her way to the airport to fly back to her home in the Midwest. We had a great conversation about the artist and the necklace, and she bought it on the spot. I wrote up the sale, and walked to the back room to wrap the necklace for her. Imagine my horror when I realized we were out of jewelry boxes and bags. The client was irritated that we had no convenient way for her to transport the jewelry home, and I was embarrassed by our lack of preparation.

Make sure that you have boxes, bags, and bubble wrap sufficient to pack everything you might sell — assume you are going to sell out, and prepare accordingly. Presenting oneself as a true professional is of paramount importance to the success of one's business.

Accept Credit Cards

The majority of our sales are paid with a credit card. Checkbooks are fading into the past, as there are fewer reasons to make the effort to write a check. If you are unable to process credit cards, you are creating an inconvenience to your customers, and are potentially limiting your sales.

In recent months, it has become much simpler to accept credit card transactions. One used to have to go through an extensive application process, purchase or lease expensive credit card machines, pay heavy transaction fees, and render monthly service fees; but he can now easily and inexpensively process credit card transactions using a smartphone.

I recently began using Square™ (visit www.squareup.com for information on how the company works) to process sales made outside the gallery. Square™ sent me a free card reader that plugs into my phone, and I can now get instant approval for sales while with the client. Intuit™, and several other providers, offer similar services – just do a Google search for "mobile credit card processing". Make sure to read all of the fine print in order to understand how the process works and to determine how long it takes for funds to clear the bank.

In today's world, there really is no excuse to not accept credit card transactions.

Love Your Clients

I recently met an artist and was having a pleasant conversation, when somehow our talk turned to the present state of the economy. I'm not sure how we got there, but suddenly the artist was confiding her deep distrust of the wealthy. She believed that they were destroying the nation and oppressing the poor. She vehemently expressed her prediction that the rich were eventually going to "get what they had coming to them".

I don't doubt the sincerity of the artist's feelings; who am I to say she is wrong in her rational? However, I couldn't help noting the irony that the same group of people against whom she railed were the very people upon whom she relied to purchase her artwork. I wonder how effective she could possibly be in working with her potential customers, when holding such vitriolic assumptions about them.

If your ultimate desire is to make sales, it behooves you to make a conscious decision to build positive relationships with each and every viewer of your work. You need to set aside any prejudices, develop sensitivity to your customer's needs, and avoid anything and everything that might offend.

Selling art is one of the few remaining businesses in which the personal relationship still reigns supreme. Of course the artwork itself is important, but of equal importance is the relationship you will establish and nurture with your customer. A positive rapport with a buyer leads to sales, and to the promise of repeat sales over a lifetime.

Drop Your Prejudices

Step one in making ready to interact with buyers is to drop any prejudices. You may have strong opinions about the world and the people in it, opinions which you have formulated through your life experiences. When you are in a selling posture, however, it is time to lock those opinions away in a deep vault. When engaged with a client, be of the mindset that allows for no thought of race, creed, color, political party, religion, sexual orientation, or socio-economic status. Each potential buyer is simply a person interested in art.

My gallery has provided me the opportunity to meet people from every walk of life and from every corner of the world. I like to think that this interaction has broadened my mind, and helped me shed most of my prejudices. I have found that there are more similarities than differences among members of the human race.

Never Pre-Judge: Everyone Is a Potential Buyer

Another danger confronting one in selling art is a complacency that grows over time with the experience of working with many customers. A salesperson develops a sense (often a false sense) of who will and who will not buy art. He thinks that he can spot a buyer by her appearance from a mile away, and that he can smell a phony from even farther.

This "expertise" one fancies he has acquired in recognizing a buyer often takes on "scientific" proportions. I remember working with someone in the business who insisted that a person carrying a camera or wearing a fanny pack was never going to buy artwork. At first, the theory seemed plausible. After all, wealthy people, the people who bought art, didn't need a camera to record the experience. The hypothesis was that they were too busy having the experiences to pause to take pictures. If a qualified buyer wanted to remember the artwork, he wouldn't need to capture its image on film: he would simply purchase the coveted piece. Someone carrying a camera was more likely an artist or a tourist. True to the same line of deduction, a person of means would never be caught dead wearing a fanny pack. Fanny packs are meant for the masses.

Initially, the theory made a lot of sense to me, but I now believe that for my co-worker, it had become a self-fulfilling prophecy. It meant that (whether consciously or unconsciously) he was treating people who fit a particular profile in a particular way; he was not giving his full effort to serve them. It made it easy to say, as the person left the gallery,

"See. They never buy. Which just goes to show my theory is iron clad. The proof is in the pudding."

At some point I realized the folly of this dogma, and determined that I was going to make it my personal mission in life to sell art to people carrying cameras, as well as to those wearing fanny packs. I have since sold art to many camera-toting buyers, and though I have yet to sell to anyone sporting a fanny pack, I'll not give up trying. My fondest dream is to sell to someone who carries his camera in his fanny pack.

Guess what else I have learned? Not everyone who drives a Porsche automatically buys art, and conversely, some folks who drive cars at the bottom of the prestige ladder are art devotees and lifelong collectors. They decided long ago how they would spend their money.

Any "expertise" you employ in pre-judging your customers is more likely to hurt your sales record than to help it. Treat everyone you encounter as an "equal opportunity" buyer. Give everything you've got to each and every camera-toting, fanny-pack-wearing tourist. Hey, just live by the Golden Rule. Enough said.

No Politics / No Religion / No Sports

Do not engage your customers in conversations about politics, religion, or sports. These topics are toxic to your efforts to make a sale. Bringing them up in any context diminishes your chance of making a sale. Because you will likely not see eye-to-eye with regard to these subjects, it is best to avoid them altogether. Why risk destroying the positive inroads you have made in the relationship?

Even if you are on the same mental wavelength with your client, be aware that these subjects are hot-button topics that will likely stir up unwanted passion. Once the blood is up, it is almost impossible to shift back to thinking about art. While politics, religion, and sports tend to evoke raw emotion, art elicits a more refined passion, one which can be negatively suppressed by a vehement diatribe.

Because distracting your clients with an inappropriate line of discourse is counter-productive to your purpose to sell art, refrain from doing so not only in your face-to-face contacts, but also in any medium where it might be encountered by potential buyers. Use caution when you post information on FaceBook™. Be wary of what you share on your blog. It is best to be circumspect in all avenues of communication and in all interactive settings.

People Don't Want You to Sell Them Something, But Are Happy to Have You Help Them Buy.

Selling art to a client can be approached in several ways. You might look at the benefit to be derived from the transaction, and push forward with the determination to succeed, no matter the cost. I suggest you will be more successful in the long run if you forget yourself and your own desires, and strive to meet the needs of your customers. By focusing on your customers' needs rather than your own, and striving to provide the highest level of service, you will transform them into life-long devotees, as well as collectors of your work.

I've met artists and gallerists who insist that salesmanship is a mystical art. They believe that one must learn its secrets in order to enchant unsuspecting customers to buy, sometimes against their will. This view of salesmanship can lead to a sense of remorse each time a sale is made; it's as though the client were swindled out of his hard-earned money. Looking at salesmanship this way is negative and unfulfilling.

I like to remember that when a sale is made, the client walks away from the transaction with a wonderful piece of artwork she will enjoy for a lifetime – all I walk away with is money; money that will be spent and forgotten before the month is out. By looking at a sale in this light, I acknowledge my duty to do everything necessary to resolve concerns, and to help the client achieve a happy outcome. Should I fail, the customer walks away with her money, but misses out on the enjoyment she would have derived from owning the artwork.

Build a Relationship of Trust

With all of this in mind, it's time to think of every encounter as an opportunity to build a lifelong relationship with your customer. A relationship is about communication, service, and trust. If you are able to establish a rapport such that your client feels she can rely upon and trust you without hesitation, she will come back again and again.

The overriding theme of this chapter can be succinctly expressed: for a collector, the decision to buy is partly about the art, but is mostly about the relationship. This fact becomes more inherent with each succeeding purchase.

CHAPTER 2 | INTRODUCTIONS

The Critical Minute

The first 60 seconds of any encounter are critical in establishing the tone of the interaction. Have you heard it said that you don't get a second chance to make a first impression? I'm not sure that adage is 100% true, but you certainly want to launch your sales efforts with your best foot forward.

Your goals during the first minute are elementary: You want to introduce yourself to the client, as well as the artwork the client will presently see. You are intent upon sending a clear message to the client that you are interested in him, that you are fully engaged, and that you are standing ready to help him in any way he needs.

It proves to be highly effective when you manage to pack a lot of energy and enthusiasm into these first 60 seconds. The road to success begins with that first, confident step; make it a power step, and follow it with a resolute gait throughout your exchange with the patron.

Smile!

I have visited many art festivals over the years. Let me describe a stereotypical encounter with a particular breed of artist. I call this breed the "Eeyore Artist". Chances are good that you know a number of artists who fit the bill (not you, of course). This artist might be male or female, young or old – it doesn't seem to matter. For this artist, everything is always going wrong, and he isn't satisfied until he's had an opportunity to complain about it.

It's always too hot or too cold – and you can guarantee it's going to rain and hail if this artist is around. He is forever remonstrating that this is his worst year ever, and that this art show is the worst show ever. A black cloud is hanging over his head, threatening to burst with a downpour to soak not only him, but anyone who has drawn near.

When customers approach, this surly artist glances up from his book, and if he perceives it's worth his time, he will let out a quick, "Let me know if you have any questions." That's it, folks. That is the extent of his sales effort. It should not come as a surprise when he has but a few lackluster sales to his credit.

Yes, you undoubtedly know precisely the type of artist I have described. He would be better served to recognize that enthusiasm and excitement are contagious, and that nothing conveys these attributes so well as a large, warm smile. Smiling lets customers know they are welcome, and that you are friendly and approachable. There is no excuse to make a festival attendee feel unwelcome, less-than, inferior to, or somehow unworthy of the artist's undivided attention.

If it has been a long time since you last smiled, it will perhaps be painful when you first start to exercise those underused muscles; but it won't kill you, I promise. The dividends will make any discomfort well worth the agony. Remember: "You're never fully dressed without a smile."

Ask If They've Seen the Art Before

Over the years, I have developed a fairly good memory for names and faces (more on that in the following pages). I can almost always remember whether I have met someone previously, and often recall the context and outcome of the first meeting. The problem is that little word - "almost" - in the preceding sentence. I "almost always" remember someone. In a gallery setting, where I am meeting and interacting with hundreds of customers each month, it is tantamount to impossible to remember each and every person with whom I have conversed.

When I engage people walking through the front door, the last thing I want to do is immediately launch into a lengthy introduction of myself and my artists. What if they are already familiar with the gallery? The worst scenario for this faux pas would be my starting a spiel with customers who have made large purchases with us in the past; they would undoubtedly expect me to remember them.

To avoid these embarrassing blunders, I have devised a simple technique which I apply each time I greet a visitor. When the customer walks through the front door of my gallery, I say:

"Good afternoon! How are you today?"

They generally respond with a much-used reply, such as:

"Very well, thank you," or "Just fine, thanks."

I then say:

"That's good to hear! Have you been in the gallery before?"

Obviously, the ideal situation is one in which I readily know the answer to this question, without having to ask it. However, when that is not the case, I don't anticipate that anybody will be annoyed by my query; not even a former client.

If a client has not been in the gallery before, this question is the perfect opportunity for me to welcome her to the gallery, and transition to my introduction. If she has been in before, it is an opportunity to welcome her back, and to start a conversation about her previous visit.

In those instances where I learn the visitor is in fact a return buyer, I apologize for failing to remember her. I don't want to make a big deal out of it – then she and I are made to feel uncomfortable. I simply say: "I am sorry I didn't recognize you right away. It's a pleasure to have you back. How may I help you?"

Introduce Yourself
This Is No Time for Humility

Once I've gotten a sense of whether or not the client has been in the gallery before, I introduce myself (or re-introduce myself, as the case may be). My introduction is straight-forward:

"Welcome! My name is Jason, I own the gallery."

Simple and succinct. I am immediately accomplishing two important jobs with this introduction – I am making the en-counter personal by giving the client my name, and I am let-ting him know the person with whom he is dealing. When dealing with me, he is working directly with the owner and decision-maker, and I want him to be aware of that right away.

Introductions are no time for false humility. If you are the artist, say so. You might think your identity should be obvious. However, the patron won't risk embarrassment by assuming something that may not be true. So in order to avoid any clumsy missteps, you must quickly let him know who you are.

This approach helps facilitate the creation of a strong connection between artist and collector.

If you are the spouse of the artist (and I happen to know there are a good many of you reading this book), I suggest you introduce yourself at the outset as the artist's business manager, or as her spouse and business manager. It is imperative to establish as much authority as you can muster. A client is more likely to take his visit seriously, and to respond to your efforts to move him to a sale, if he sees you are a decision maker and an integral member of the team.

What if you are not the spouse, not a decision maker, nor a business manager? What if you are a newly hired gallery employee with next to no authority? We've all been there at some point; after all, one has to begin somewhere. Ask the gallery owner how she would like you to introduce yourself. Sometimes the gallery can give you a title – "Director of _____" sounds nice. "Associate" will work as well. If you do not have a title, don't be concerned. Merely act like you own the place, and introduce yourself with confidence.

To The Gallery Owner

Give your employees a title, and as much authority as you deem you can comfortably cede. Your staff will be more effective if they have the authority to close sales, and a title to establish that authority with customers.

The title is the easy part – Director of Sales, Gallery Director, Senior Associate – each does the trick nicely. Giving the actual authority can be more difficult. As business owners, we are ultimately responsible for everything that happens in the gallery and every decision that is made. Some owners want to be directly involved in every decision, especially when it comes to negotiating (See Chapter 9 | Negotiate!). You will find, however, that sales increase when you empower your employees to act on their own within the parameters you set for them. The more flexibility they have to offer special services and to negotiate, the more effective they will be in working with customers and selling to customers.

Ask for the Client's Name

Now that the client knows who you are, it's time for you to find out who she is. Often upon introducing yourself, the client will reciprocate with her name; if she doesn't, however, don't hesitate to ask.

A client's name is among the most valuable tools you have at your disposal when constructing a professional relationship. Trying to work without a name poses a handicap difficult to overcome. Don't let the opportunity of getting the name slip away – the first minute is the time to ask. There is no need to feel pushy or invasive, and soon enough, the practice of exchanging names will become second nature.

In the event a client fails to provide his name after I introduce myself, I simply say, "Now, tell me your name." As long as you are putting my advice into action with a smile, no one should be affronted. It is more than likely that you will receive both the name and a handshake.

You will find that getting the name becomes the easy part: remembering the name . . . well, that's a different story. Remembering (and using) a name is so important that the next chapter, in its entirety, is devoted solely to the subject. For now, let us assume you've gotten the name, and focus on the final thing that needs to happen in your first minute with a buyer.

Give the Client a Brief Introduction to the Art

Now that the client knows who you are, and you know his name, it's time to help him understand what he can expect to experience as he peruses your art.

What you say about your art makes a real difference in the level of interest a purchaser will show, as well as in how he will experience the art. Compose the introduction carefully, and write it down, listing the points you wish to make and using the words which will best illustrate them. Practice the scripted introduction until you are comfortable enough to present it in real time.

This provides yet another opportunity to toot your own horn if you are the artist, or to praise the quality of the art you are exhibiting if you are a gallerist. Once again, this is no time to be falsely modest. If you have won awards for your work, been featured in magazines, or sold to important collectors, now is the time to mention these accolades.

If there is a particular theme to the work the collector will be seeing, let him know what the theme is and why you were drawn to the subject. He will be interested to learn what inspired your work; this information adds an intangible, albeit intrinsic value to the art.

The introduction should be kept brief, and viewed as a chance to grab the visitor's attention and to bring focus to his experience. The last thing you want is for this to be an unproductive and forgettable encounter; the first moments in "meeting and greeting" play a major role in determining the outcome of the event.

CHAPTER 3 | WHAT'S IN A NAME?

No More Excuses

"I'm so sorry. I'm terrible with names. Tell me your name again?"

Everyone has forgotten a name: It happens, and having forgotten, you need not feel disconcerted when you find it necessary to ask for the name again. If, however, you are constantly forgetting names, you are failing to utilize a tool that will assist you in becoming a more effective salesperson.

It has been said that the sweetest sound in any language is the sound of one's own name. When someone remembers and uses your name, you know she is paying attention to you, and that she cares about you. The use of another's name creates the personal touch that enriches what might otherwise be a sterile appointment.

If you are terrible at remembering names, it is probably the same reason you are terrible at golf, knitting, or chess. Like any other skill, remembering names is something that has to be first learned, and then practiced. Though some of us have better memories than others, it is doubtful that we were born with an innate ability to recall names. Practically anyone can develop the ability.

Repeat the Name Aloud

No more excuses – it's time for you to start remembering names! The first step is pretty obvious: start using the names. In the last chapter, I explained that during an introductory encounter, always ask for the visitors' names. Upon their reply, repeat the names. Take for instance the following example:

"I'm Bill, and this is my wife, Nancy," the visitor says.

"Bill, Nancy," you reply, "it's a pleasure to meet you."

The act of using the names starts the process of cementing those names in both your short and long-term memories, and helps your customers warm up to you. Two birds with one stone.

Run the Names Through Your Mind

If you could step into my mind during the greeting process, you would hear two things happening. At a conscious level, you would hear me engaging in conversation with my clients; at a deeper, almost sub-conscious level, you would hear this:

"Bill, Bill, Bill, Bill, Bill, Bill, Bill, Bill, Nancy, Nancy, Nancy, Nancy, Nancy, Nancy, Nancy, Nancy, Bill, Bill, Nancy, Nancy, Bill, Nancy, Bill, Nancy, Bill, Nancy, Bill, Bill, Bill, Nancy, Nancy, Nancy."

As you can plainly see, my memory is actually pretty lousy. I have to repeat a name at least ten times (twenty times is better still) if I am to have any hope at all of retaining it.

A shortcut in this process is to associate new names with the names of other people you already know. If someone introduces herself as Carrie, for example, I'm not going to have to do nearly as much work to retain the name, because all I have to do is remember, "This person has the same name as my wife."

The risk with association – and I have experienced this – is forgetting the association. The more distant the association, the greater the risk. Wouldn't you just know there would have to be some threat of peril in even the wisest council!

I recollect meeting a guest to the gallery whose name I associated with a childhood friend. This was great until several minutes into the conversation, when having used his name repeatedly, the guest finally corrected me; I then realized I had been calling him by the name of my childhood friend's brother. Hey, I was close!

Write the Names Down ASAP

The repetitive drilling of a name is a good way to get the initial grasp of a client's name. Then, if you really want to hard-wire the name into your brain and have it permanently accessible, write it down.

I will explain later in the book how my interaction with clients is a kind of dance, one in which I waltz in and out of conversation range. After I have met the customers, coaxed their names out of them, and given a brief introduction to the gallery, I step back and allow them to begin exploring the gallery.

While they start poking around, I dance my way back to my desk and write down their names. I have devised a simple form we use to add customers to our mailing list, and I use this form to record the customers' names, and to note any pertinent information I have gleaned from our initial conversations.

Once I have written names down, I own them. The mere act of writing effectively cements the names in my memory. Of course, if for some reason (sudden onset amnesia, perhaps) I do forget a name, I have only to return to my notes to be reminded.

Using Names Repeatedly
Throughout the Encounter

To make the most from the impressive recall of your clients' names, sprinkle them throughout the remainder of your conversation. Make a conscious effort to inject names into the exchange every three sentences or so.

"That's a great question," becomes, "That's a great question, Bill."

"Step up closer to the painting, Nancy, to get a better look at the brushwork."

It is nearly impossible to overuse your buyers' names. Obviously, you want the conversation to feel natural, but the more you can use names, the better.

Other Tips with Names

There is a limit to the number of names you can fit into your mind at any given moment. I sincerely hope this limit doesn't have anything to do with IQ, because my limit seems to be four. That is, if a group of four people comes into the gallery and offers introductions, with some serious effort on my part, I have a pretty good chance of remembering the four names.

If, however, the number in a party moves beyond four, I have my work cut out for me. I still ask for the names from larger groups, but I then focus on remembering only four of them, and hope I have been lucky enough to choose the names of the four folks most likely to buy.

Touch

Memorizing and using your client's name will create a sense of relationship and amity. Touching your client lightly and casually will intensify this sense of connection, and thus invite an even deeper degree of attachment.

Touching a client must be done sensitively and appropriately. You can discern how comfortable your client will be with touch when you shake his hand during the introduction — if there is no hesitation in the handshake, and it is firm and confident, you will have good reason to think that the client is comfortable having you briefly share his space.

Throughout the remainder of the visit, you can reach out and touch an arm or a shoulder to emphasize a point regarding a piece of artwork. Guide the collector to another painting by gently taking his elbow.

I spent several years in Brazil, where touch during communication is not only welcomed, but expected. While there, I became convinced that some Brazilians would be unable to communicate if their hands were tied behind their backs. Not only are they avid gesticulators, but they also reach out and touch the listener throughout a conversation to emphasize key points.

The result of a conversation with a Brazilian is that you feel as though you have never before heard a more heartfelt speech, nor connected so closely with another human being. It is an experience one is unlikely to forget.

We Americans, generally speaking, are more reserved in our inter-personal relationships. Touching is a rarity in our culture, which makes it all the more powerful when employed in establishing a relationship. Just don't overdo it. If you sense any unease in the contact, draw back immediately; after all, it's more important your that customer feels comfortable than connected. That being said, the majority of people respond positively to touch.

CHAPTER 4 | THE VALUE OF QUESTIONS

When you get right down to it, the process of getting to know someone, the process of building a relationship, is a process of asking questions. Asking questions opens the door to discovering who someone is, learning about his background, and understanding his wants and needs. Since salesmanship is a skill we employ to meet a person's needs, to become effective, we have to learn to ask the right questions.

Great questions do two things. First, they get your clients to talk about themselves. In order to get them talking about themselves, you need to ask questions that lead to more than a rudimentary "yes" or "no" answer. Your questions should be open ended, so as to encourage a more complete response; a response rich in detail. Second, great questions lead to additional questions. The goal is not to fire off a list of rote questions you ask everyone; the goal is to start a conversation. Conversations begin with questions, and the best conversations are sustained by still more questions.

The principle reason for asking questions will perhaps come as a surprise. Most people equate selling with telling. They think selling entails telling their prospective buyers the wonderful features of the product they are hocking, listing the reasons the item should be purchased, and talking a blue streak about themselves. Contrary to this line of reasoning, salesmanship is not about talking; it is about listening. If you wish to become a great salesperson, be you artist or gallerist, start asking great questions, and start listening.

I recently heard someone say (and I'm sorry, I don't remember who it was or where I heard it) that if you are talking more than 35% of the time in a sales encounter, you are never going to make the sale. While this may have the ring of an unscientific, pulled-out-of-thin-air statistic, I know the underlying principle is true – listen more than you talk. Respond to what you hear. Get out of your own way.

Six Great Questions to Break the Ice and Encourage Conversation

1. *"What brings you out today?"*

I find this particular question to be a great way to begin a conversation. By asking this question, I immediately get a sense of the intention of the guest through her response. Frequently, the response I get is something like: "Oh, we're just out looking around," or "We just thought we would get out and look at some art." Not particularly helpful responses, but at least now I know I am going to have to create the sense of urgency to buy, because the clients are not bringing their own.

Occasionally, however, I'll get a response like, "Actually, we're looking for a piece for our dining room." Now there is some valuable information! With the help of some good follow up questions, I can usually flesh out exactly what it is they are looking for, and guide them to a particular painting or sculpture.

I remember a couple who visited the gallery only six months after we opened. The couple lived in Seattle, but had recently purchased a second home in Arizona where they would spend three to four months a year, including most weekends during Spring Training.

They had already finished furnishing the house, and it was now time to refine the home with artwork – hence their visit to the gallery. After introducing myself and requesting their names, I asked:

2. *"What are you looking for in particular today?"*

"Well," said the wife, "we have a wall in our entry-way that needs a painting. It's an important wall, because you see it not only when you enter, but you also see it from the living and dining rooms."

"And what kind of painting did you have in mind?"

"We're not exactly sure," replied the husband, "but we thought perhaps a desert landscape."

"And what size do you need for the space?" I further inquired.

"It needs to be a pretty major piece," replied the wife.

With a little digging I was able to get a rough idea of the size of the wall, and I thought I had the perfect artist for them.

Though they liked the work of the artist I showed them, it was clear that none of his pieces on display were precisely right for their space. I was able, however, to go to my backroom and pull a piece by the same artist that was much larger. As soon as they saw it, they exclaimed that this was the perfect piece for their home.

I made arrangements to deliver and hang the painting, and it fit the space perfectly. The colors and content could not have been better had the artist created the piece specifically for their home.

None of this would have occurred had I not asked the simple question at the beginning of our encounter: "What brings you out today?"

3.   *"Where are you from?"*

It is exciting when you ascertain that a client is looking for something quite specific, and that you can help him satisfy that quest. More times than not, however, your customers will not have a definite purpose in mind. Art lovers will seek opportunities to explore and discover new artwork, with no precise intention. This doesn't mean they aren't going to buy –

it means your strategy should shift from a "let's get to it" orientation, to a slightly more relaxed approach.

What you now have is the opportunity to introduce the art enthusiasts to new artwork. Focus on creating an experience for them, rather than upon the possibility of making sales.

Initiating a discussion with, "Where are you from?" can be a smooth and pleasant way to break the ice. Knowing whether they are local, or visiting from elsewhere, can be useful in directing their attention to particular subjects or themes reflected in the work.

4.   *"What kind of work do you do?"*

A large part of a person's identity is tied to the work he or she does. Healthy or not, one experiences his sense of self and measures his individual worth through the work he performs. Because vocation plays such a significant role in how we see ourselves, and in the way we look at others, it makes for a ready topic for talk.

In as much as the goal is to get the client to talk about herself, ask her what kind of work she does. Be certain to ask follow up questions about the nature of her work. Don't merely ask what she does; if she is a doctor, ask about her specialty, how long she has been in practice, where she trained, etc. Keep her talking. Avoid giving the impression that she is being evaluated, or sized up, to determine her ability to make a pricey purchase.

I am curious by nature, and I find other people's lines of work fascinating. This curiosity has served me well over the years in building relationships with patrons. I'm not sure if curiosity is something that can be developed, but if you have natural curiosity, I suggest you cultivate it. If you are not innately curious, do what you must to indicate a sincere interest in the people you meet.

5. *"Tell me about your art collection."*

This is an effective request during the course of your conversation. If you can induce your clients to think and talk about past purchases, and the joy and satisfaction the art has brought into their lives, you can lead them to associate the same pleasure with their response to your work. Through such discussion, you will likely get a sense for the type of work that interests them, as well as for their true intent to expand their collections.

Collectors love talking about their collections, and they typically convey useful information as they speak. As a side note, this is an excellent reason to visit collectors' homes and to ask them to show you around. When you see the art they have previously purchased, you will be in a better position to guide their future procurements.

6. *What have you seen that has most interested you today?*

This might seem like a counter-productive question. After all, do we really want your clients thinking about other artwork they have seen? Isn't there the risk that we will push them toward something else? I have not found this to be the case.

This is yet another query that allows me to step into my customers' day, and become a part of their art experience. I will also better ascertain what interests them in a manner that simply asking them will never reveal.

At a more subtle level, however, I am encouraging them to compare and contrast the artwork they are seeing in my gallery with the work they have seen previously and elsewhere.

Through the process of asking certain questions, I am actually guiding them to thoughtfully evaluate the art.

By doing this (and this is an important point, thus I underline it) I am attempting to create a choice between something and something. In other words, I am pleased to have them compare a particular piece of art in my gallery to a piece in another gallery, if in so doing I convince them to purchase one of those two pieces today.

Sure, there is the possibility that the clients will decide that the other work of art they saw is more to their liking, and buy it; yet I still maintain that I would rather be up against another work of art than up against nothing. If it's a choice between something they're seeing in my gallery and something they've seen in another gallery, I have at least an even chance of proving my case when I use the knowledge of what I'm up against. If it's a choice between a particular piece of art and nothing, nothing will too often be elected.

Now, if I truly do have my clients' best interests at heart, I am going to encourage them to purchase the piece of artwork which best meets those interests, even when that piece must be purchased from a competing gallery. Fortunately, through the exercise of doing the comparing and contrasting and eva-luating, together with my considered in-put, the outcome is usually going to be to my advantage. In other words, if I can get involved in the clients' decision process, and help them to discover the positive aspects of the art they are seeing in my gallery, and how they outweigh those of the art they have seen previously, I am likely to win the sale. If not, I don't de-serve the sale, and they will be better served elsewhere.

I know what you are thinking at this point: "Seriously? You would send clients to buy art from another gallery?" The an-swer is yes: I would, and sometimes do. Nothing lets the clients know my sincerity in assisting them to meet their needs like encouraging them to make a purchase that will not benefit me. If I have succeeded in helping them, I like to think that the next time they are in the area, mine will be the first gallery they visit. Why? Because they know they can trust me unequivocally.

Avoid Dead-End Questions

As previously asserted, the goal in asking questions is to get your customer talking. Notice the questions I have suggested are open-ended; that is, they encourage the customer to give answers which can readily be expanded and expounded.

Asking questions that can be answered with "yes" or "no" will invariably lead to brief and awkward dialogue:

"Do you live here?"

"No."

"You're visiting from out of town?"

"Yes."

"Are you here on vacation?"

"No."

"Business?"

"Yup."

You get the picture. Much better to ask an open-ended question:

(1) "Where do you live?"

(2) "What brings you here?" or

(3) "How are you enjoying our beautiful weather?"

Ask Follow Up Questions

Questions propel a conversation, but they are only starters. Don't ask these questions in order, one after the other. Typically, one or two queries should suffice to open a dialogue that will take on a natural life of its own.

An effective way to keep a conversation going is to listen intently to what the client is saying, and ask thoughtful follow up questions. Keep the customer talking. For example, if she states she is from St. Louis, ask how long she has been there, what took her there, and what she likes about the city. When you learn a person's profession (as in the example of the doctor), ask for details about her area of expertise, and how she found her way into that line of work.

This process of interacting with clients and engaging them in conversation will take very little effort on your part – it's easy to get people to talk about themselves. The real work comes as you strive to analyze what they have said, and incorporate the resulting insights into your sales efforts. The more information you garner, the more effective your assistance, and the more bountiful your returns.

CHAPTER 5 | CREATE AN EXPERIENCE

Shopping for art is unlike any other genre of consumer experience. Most shopping is motivated by necessity, or at least by the perception of necessity; it constitutes a robotic trek to the grocery store, to the mall, or to the office supply. You know you need something, you figure out where to obtain it, and you venture out to get it. I would like to think that art is as critical to life as food or raiment, but I have yet to hear reported a fatality resulting from aesthetic starvation, or cultural deprivation. Because art is a luxury and one of life's great pleasures, shopping for it should be an experience of abundant joy.

Strive to Create a Pleasant and Memorable Experience for Your Buyers

Display your art in a clean, uncluttered space. Make sure that each work of art has sufficient space. A common mistake made by both galleries and studios is the cluttering of display space with too much art. Offering too many choices in too small an area can create confusion and chaos, and engender

81

uncertainty in a client's mind. Showing too much art also diminishes the relative importance to be appreciated in each piece.

Provide your customers with creature comforts to make extended viewing of the entire array enjoyable; refreshments, seating (if possible), and climate control. It would be unfortunate to lose a customer simply because she is uncomfortable in your space.

Set the tone for the meeting with appropriate music. Choose music that elevates the mood without distracting from the experience. I pay a lot of attention to the essential vibrations of my customers, and try to play the music they would choose to hear, were they in charge of making the selection.

Tell a Story

A patron's initial response to your work is going to be raw and emotional. At a basic level, he will apprehend immediately whether or not he likes the work. If he does like the work, your job is to reinforce the positive connection, and to build the interest into an overwhelming, irresistible desire to buy.

Capturing the customer's attention and imagination will imbue a sense of ownership in the piece, and nothing will engage the mind so well as a good story. Take him on a brief journey to unfold your interest in the subject matter, to elucidate the creation process, and to share your wonder at the miraculous result. Let your enthusiasm be contagious.

Here is a persuasive first step: If the piece of art is a landscape, talk about the setting in nature where the painting was created. The information satisfying the following questions will provide the fodder for your story:

- What drew you to the area?

- Had you been there before?

- How did you get there?

- Was the setting what you expected?

- How long did you stay?

- What most surprised you about the landscape of the area?

- What aspects of the landscape were you most interested in capturing in your painting?

- What most excites you about the painting?

- What response did you hope to elicit through the painting?

Similarly, if you have created a figurative sculpture, you could address the following interrogatories to create a narrative:

- Which gestures were you interested in capturing?

- What did you have to do to get the model to convey those gestures?

- What was the most difficult or challenging aspect of capturing the gestures?

- What most excites you about the piece you have created?

- To what should the viewer pay special attention?

What if you are an abstract painter? How much story can you extract from an abstract painting? Answer these questions and see where the story takes you:

- How much did you know about the piece before you began?

- What emotion was primarily driving the composition?

- What struggles did you face as you worked on the piece, and how did you overcome them?

- What surprised you about the way the piece came together?

- What aspect or detail of the work most excites you?

- How does this piece fit into the narrative of the other pieces you are creating? Does it say something new? Does it build on a theme?

You get the idea. Asking yourself these kinds of questions in advance, and sharing the answers in an improvised narrative at the appropriate time, will help the client begin to engage more fully with your work. The personal touch of the creator is arguably the most efficacious tool, after the paint brush, in effectuating a sale.

Some would argue that your story might get in the way of the client formulating his own interpretation regarding the work, and that you might actually hinder his connecting to the piece. Is it possible to share too much information? Can the collector feel bombarded with all the relevant detail? I have never found this to be the case. A customer is going to bring his own story and exposition to the piece, no matter what you do; your chronicle only adds panache to the experience.

For Example . . .

I work with an artist who does an amazing job of narrating each piece he creates. Upon completing a work of art, he sits down and writes his narrative. The narrative is a couple of paragraphs long at most, but it demonstrates to an art collector that the artist is focused and deliberate in the creation of his work. There is "method in his madness." There is "grist for his genius."

This particular artist's work is figurative and often involves multiple figures in relationships: the relationship between husband and wife, father and child, among sisters, etc. The relationships become the subject of the work and the driving force behind the compositions.

I have witnessed tears forming in the eyes of clients reading his descriptions. It is not difficult to move the clients to buy when they have felt that kind of connection to a piece.

Educate

During the course of speaking about your artwork, you have an opportunity to expound upon your influences. Many art collectors love to talk about art history, their favorite artists, and their preferred art movements and styles. If you can place your work in a context with the great masters, and explain where and how the piece fits into the succession of art history, you will enable the collector to better apprehend and more fully appreciate your work.

Point out both the similarities of and the differences between your work and your influences. Indicate the details in your work that support your claims. The placement of your creation within the "fold of the famed" adds an extra measure of weight, authenticity, and credibility.

You can also educate the buyer about the process of creating the piece. Sharing specific technical know-how and methodology invites her to feel she is an insider. It also prepares her to explain the process to those who will ooh and aah about her purchase when she displays it in her home.

As you talk about the technical aspects of the art, tread the line carefully between getting too technical, and not giving your client enough credit. Never speak down to, nor patronize her. At the same time, do avoid using "art world" jargon and getting too esoteric about the work itself, and the inspiration behind it.

Treat Each Work as a Masterpiece

This truism will be emphasized throughout the book: The collector has the right to be convinced that the particular piece in which he is interested is among the best and most important works of art you have produced.

"Bill, I'm glad you noticed this piece," you will say. "This is one of my most important pieces. Of course, I strive to create a masterpiece each time I step into the studio, but let me show you why this particular piece is so special."

When handling the artwork – moving it to a new spot so a client can better see the piece, for example – don a pair of white kid gloves. The effect of wearing gloves is dramatic (try it if you don't believe it), as suddenly this work of art becomes museum worthy because it is being handled with the deference given a museum piece.

Invite Touch

There is tremendous advantage in empowering a potential collector to experience the artwork with as many senses as possible. Of course, sight is the obvious sense brought into play as the painting is examined both up close, and at a distance.

The senses of hearing and smell play essential roles at an imaginary level. If you are a landscape painter, for example, you might suggest that the client step into the scene and hear the breeze blowing through the trees, and smell the fresh scent of pine needles in the air.

The sense of touch is too often overlooked as a means through which an art enthusiast is able to make a literal connection to an art piece. Contrary to everything museum curators and gallery owners tell their visitors, if I have a client whom I deem to be sincerely interested in a piece, I will invite him to touch it.

Touching comes naturally when dealing with sculpture – in fact, a principle element of the experience can become tactile when the client is invited to explore the contours of the sculpture. A careful caress will not cause any damage, but will facilitate a degree of connection to the object of his interest.

I don't limit touching to sculpture, however. If I have a patron interested in a painting, I invite her to lightly touch the surface of the painting. I can hear the gasps! This sort of activity calls into question the wisdom of the sages throughout the ages. Nevertheless, in certain situations, under supervision, touching is both appropriate and effective. Getting a client to touch the artwork creates not only the perception of connection, but also of ownership. Once she has touched it, the artwork becomes more tangible, more real. Now she must give it her full attention. She is invested.

Mention that you don't allow just anyone to touch the work, but that you want her to feel the texture of the surface of the piece. Show her how to touch the painting, and if you are comfortable doing so, guide her hand. When a sculpture is the item of interest, let her feel the cool exterior of the sculpture, and get a notion of its heft.

Giving a collector an opportunity to experience art through the miracle of the senses makes for a lovely afternoon; but more to the point, it showcases your acumen as an astute salesperson. Chances are good that she is now determined to make the piece her own, and to enjoy it in her home.

Go the Extra Mile

The age we live in allows us to take advantage of diverse media as we seek to provide experiences for our customers to connect with art. Never has it been so easy to create multi-media presentations to enrich the client's understanding of the artist and the artwork, and to deepen his appreciation. With minimal effort and expense, video, audio, and online informational resources can be created.

We recently put on a show for a husband and wife artist team we represent. The artists work together to create their paintings, each working on specific areas of the same canvas. Because we like to share with guests the couple's unusual approach to creating their art, we thought it would be interesting and helpful to provide more insight into their artistic process.

We arranged a visit to the artists' studio, and recorded a video tour of their workspace. We invited the artists to talk about each of the pieces to be featured in the show. We then made posts of the video available on our website, and displayed barcodes in our gallery that could be scanned by Smartphone to access the video.

While it would be impossible to calculate the precise impact these efforts had on sales, we did receive a good deal of positive feedback. Putting the video together gave my staff and me a deeper insight into this fascinating couple, and a better understanding of the means by which they produce their paintings. It made us better advocates for their work.

Remember, the goal is to help the client feel that she is purchasing the pièce de résistance from your career inventory. Making the extra effort to present her with the details will emphasize the superiority of her purchase.

CHAPTER 6 | CREATE A VISION

The process of cultivating interest in an art piece culminates in the customer's imagining that he owns the piece. The proficient salesperson orchestrates a pleasurable experience for the buyer. She directs the exploration of the art; she encourages the visualization of the piece in the customer's home or place of business; she elicits the joyous anticipation of personal possession. She "artfully" and deftly effectuates the sale.

Find a Space for the Artwork

Early in my selling career, I remember asking a customer:

"Do you have a place for this piece?"

"No, we really don't. We've been buying artwork for decades, and now every wall is full."

"Oh, I see. Oh, my, that poses a real problem, then, doesn't it?"

It proved to be an awkward and unproductive exchange of words. With my limited experience, I had no idea how to proceed.

On another occasion, I asked the same question. The customer seemed offended by my query, and made a rather emphatic retort:

"We don't buy art that way. If we love a piece, we will *find* a space for it."

Though my purpose in asking this question was justified, my phrasing was obviously inept.

My goal back then was the same goal I have today: Encourage the client to start the task of figuring precisely where she is going to place the art. This is actually a worthy exercise to initiate because once she is mentally searching for the ideal space, she is no longer pondering the issue of whether or not she should buy the piece. Now that she has settled the problem of placement, the opportunity is ripe to move in and close the sale (see Chapter 7 | Go for the Close).

While I appreciate the sentiment of my client who let me know that when she likes a piece she is going to buy it and find a space for it, the fact is that ultimately *every* client will need to find a spot for the art. Because it must be displayed somewhere, it is best to address the issue of placement at the outset, and to offer the benefit of my expertise in solving the challenge.

Since those early experiences, I have rephrased my question. I now ask: "Where would you place this piece?" As is evident, the question in this form inspires the customer to mentally address the issue, and diverts any notion that there might be an unsolvable problem.

Occasionally, even after my best effort, a customer will still protest that she simply does not have space for the art. My response to both that and other protestations will be covered in another chapter (Chapter 8 | Resolve Concerns). It suffices to say at this point that the customer does need to be encouraged to consider the logistics of adding the art piece to her collection.

Engage the Client's Imagination

Once a space has been found for the objet d'art, it is time to ask:

"What will the piece do for this room?"

"What will the vivid colors in this piece do for the room?"

"What will the drama of this piece do for your room?"

When the art enthusiast has mentally envisioned the piece in a space of his own choosing, he is well down the path to making it a part of his collection. He acknowledges that it will be shown to its best advantage in his home. Why, in his mind, it is as though he himself commissioned it!

Yet another aspect of the art's impact in its new space is worth consideration. Though the art is purchased to bring pleasure to the buyer, a measure of satisfaction is also anticipated in the positive response he expects to elicit when he shares the art with visitors to his home. Family, friends, and business associates will admire his exquisite taste.

"Many of my clients tell me my work becomes a real focal point in a room," the artist declares. "Think of the impact this painting (or sculpture) will have when your family or friends come into the room and see it for the first time."

I've found that the more fully I engage the imagination, the greater the sense of ownership. Thus, if there are particular aspects of the work that are unique, I like to emphasize those aspects in guiding my client to picture the work in his home. I point out that some of my artists create amazing results by employing vivid colors that actually change, depending upon the light. I invite the buyer to visualize the painting in various lighting conditions – morning, full light, dusk, and the dark of night. I inquire about the lighting in the room.

My objective is to get the client to help me step into the room with him. I request the dimensions of the room, information about the furnishings, and descriptions of the accessories and objets d'art.

Speak with the Assumption that the Sale Is a Reality—Speak Assumptively

As the discourse with the collector continues, I eventually make a subtle shift and begin to speak of the artwork as though it is already his. I refer to the canvas as "your painting", or to the bronze as "your sculpture".

I reflect upon the joyous experience he is going to have with the item in a manner which assumes he has made the decision to purchase. "When you hang this piece, notice how the light at various times of the day can dramatically affect the mood and tone of the piece," I suggest.

In keeping with all of the steps already suggested in this chapter, finding a space for the item of art and engaging the client's imagination while speaking to him in an assumptive manner, are two more steps in moving him toward a sense of implied ownership. These measures are effective when taken by the confident and competent salesperson, be she an artist or a gallerist.

Chapter 7 | Go for the Close

Now that the client is genuinely interested in a piece of artwork, and is thoroughly informed with regard to its background and source of inspiration, the time is ripe to formally commit him to the purchase. Easier said than done.

I have watched both artists and salespeople participate in the most promising interactive exercise, only to fail at the critical moment to ask the potential buyer for the sale. It is then no surprise when the client walks away without having made the purchase. It is rare, indeed, when the customer decides to buy without having been asked. Many sales are lost simply because the client is never given the opportunity to buy.

I understand that asking for the sale can be the most intimidating part of the sales process. There is the perception of risk associated with prompting the customer to "get on with it".

What if he says no?

What if he has just been playing along, and doesn't actually like the art?

What if he thinks the artwork is too expensive?

What if he isn't ready to buy now?

These are all valid possibilities, and they pose potential problems. If you don't ask for the sale, however, you will never know why the client isn't buying; you will only know that he is not. Better to ask for the sale, and have your client decline, so that you can move forward to remedy the problems which are hindering the sale.

Ask for the Close

A moment will arrive (I like to call it "the moment of truth") when you have given all the information you can give about the piece, and the client is primed to buy. This moment typically comes immediately after you have elicited a positive comment, and there follows a brief moment of silence.

Take a deep breath, and ask for the close.

There are a number of questions you can ask to effectuate the sale. My favorites are:

"Shall I write that up for you?"

"Would you like to take it home?"

"Would you like to do it?"

This is the one time I use a question to elicit a simple "yes" or "no" response. I want to make it clear that I am asking for the sale; and frankly, I want to put the customer on the spot.

I have been on the buyer's side of this encounter, and know firsthand what is going on in his mind and body when asked directly for the sale. All logic and reason fly right out the window. A primal need for decisive action is aroused. The heart rate quickens. Adrenaline starts pumping, and raw emotion bubbles up to the surface. Psychologically and physiologically, it becomes imperative to answer with a resounding "yes"!

With a "no", the shopper must justify his refusal to buy. He must withstand the salesperson's counter arguments. He must give some sort of explanation as to why he has let things go so far.

The merciful salesperson will suggest that a "maybe", rather than an outright "no", might prove to be the most advantageous response for everyone concerned. After all, "no" is final. Better to leave things open-ended for the possibility of further exploration.

This rationale draws the focus to what is taking place in the "here-and-now". The long-term ramifications of the sale, should it happen, can be considered "if-and-when".

I know what you are thinking; this all sounds a bit on the high pressure side, and the last thing you want to do is come across like a used car salesman. I am certainly not suggesting that you utilize the tactics for clearing a used car lot. If, however, a customer requires your exertion to get what he wants, you owe it to him to ask for the close.

I have rarely had a customer disappointed because he bought a work of art; I have had many customers express regret that they didn't buy something they truly loved, but instead allowed it to slip away. The job of a salesperson is to do everything he can to help the client overcome perceived obstacles that stand in the way of purchasing your art. Often, the client himself is the greatest obstacle, and requires a gentle shove to get out of his own way.

Obviously, many lookers manage to raise legitimate concerns, and to say a firm "no, thank you" when asked for the sale. Still, there exists a proven psychological advantage to be gained by asking for the sale. It may be surprising that the collector will sometimes respond with an unexpected, "Yes, let's do it", all because the interaction has proven positive. When he has been thoroughly informed about the artist and the work, and duly impressed by their significance, most obstacles can be readily overcome.

I will first deal with the happy outcome, the successful sale, and then dive into practical responses to concerns or objections the client might raise. Looking at a myriad of possible scenarios will allow the salesperson, be he artist, agent, or gallerist, to procure the desired sale.

Wrap It Up – Literally

In the instance that a collector responds affirmatively to the invitation to purchase, the salesperson's heart inevitably races in harmony with hers. Hearing a client say "yes" is one of the most thrilling experiences of this business. But do resist the urge to party. Just because the buyer has agreed to make the purchase does not mean the work is finished. In fact, at this moment there lurks a grave threat: Buyer's Remorse.

Although mentioned earlier, the delayed contrition for acquisition is rare. Unfortunately, buyer's remorse is a very real monster hiding out in the back of many buyers' minds. It conceals itself, waiting for a major purchase, and the moment the transaction is made, it immediately commences to growl all sorts of doubts and misgivings:

"What if you made a mistake?" the monster whispers.

"You shouldn't be spending this much money."

"Maybe you don't like it as much as you thought."

"What will other people think?"

Though these doubts might manifest directly before the sale is initiated, they are strongest during the fleeting moments preceding the closing of the deal. I have seen sales destroyed because the salesperson hesitated to step in and slay the beast.

The best insurance against the burgeoning of buyer's remorse is to straightway move the client from the decision to purchase into the mechanical process of writing up the sale. As soon as I receive a positive response to an invitation to purchase, I immediately move the client to my desk to do the paperwork.

As we're walking to the desk I ask, "Will we be shipping (or delivering if the client lives in the area) the artwork to your home?" The timing of this question serves to shift the client's mind away from the actual purchase (when buyer's remorse can start eating away at him), to the logistical matters which are easy to handle.

Begin filling out the sales slip by asking for the client's address, phone number, and email. Inquire as to whether the information might be implemented for purposes of tracking the shipment of the artwork.

Throughout the process of writing up the sale, continue to engage the customer in a dialogue requiring feedback, thus leaving as little silence as possible. Silence and reflection give the Beast a chance to come out.

Finally, give the client his total and ask whether he would like to pay by credit card, cash, or check (credit card is today's preferred option). The client will know what to do next.

The process of writing up the sale, and then handling all of the logistics of getting the artwork to the client's home, are essential steps in completing the transaction. Take care of the details quickly, competently, and professionally.

Upon handing the client his receipt, stand, extend your hand, and congratulate him on his fine purchase. Compliment him on his good taste.

"Congratulations. You've demonstrated great instincts in your selection. I know you are going to enjoy this piece for many years to come. Thank you for your business!"

Notice I don't thank the buyer specifically for purchasing the artwork; rather, I congratulate and thank him for his business. As I mentioned before, it is imperative that he believes he is the one who is coming out ahead in the transaction. If I thank the client for buying the artwork, it is tantamount to my saying that it is I who has benefited most from the sale.

Don't Try to Close too Early

Timing is a big part of the closing procedure. While it is a mistake to not try to close when the opportunity presents itself, it can be disastrous to try to close too soon. The patron needs to be properly primed.

Asking for the close is a proven sales strategy, but it is not magic. The attempt to push a close each time a person hesitates in front of a piece of art will ultimately push him right out the door.

A move to close should come only when the client has expressed genuine interest in a piece, and only after he has had the chance to learn its background. The salesperson should have ascertained that there exists a particular space for this particular piece. It is to no one's advantage to make anyone feel unduly rushed.

Don't False Close

Don't close on a note that gives the client an excuse not to make the decision to purchase now. When a client is actively interested in a piece of artwork, there can be a real temptation on the part of the salesperson to offer photos of the art, along with a brochure and business card. However, one must realize that if she gives in to this urge, she is implying the client shouldn't buy now, but should instead go home and think about it. Sending a hesitant buyer out the door to "think about it" is a virtual guarantee the sale will never happen. Remember, once a client leaves, the chance of his returning to purchase the art is remote at best.

I'm not implying that one shouldn't follow up with the client who is unwilling to commit (See Chapter 10); I simply want to encourage the artist or gallerist to make every effort to close the sale today. Do not provide the purchaser with a ready excuse to delay.

Make it a policy to offer a brochure or photo of a piece of artwork only when every other means to transact a sale has been exhausted. Most successful transactions will occur in the here-and-now, rather than sometime in the nebulous future.

CHAPTER 8 | RESOLVE CONCERNS

You will be most effective in making sales if you put every effort into helping your customer resolve his own concerns. Asking for the close will often lead directly to the sale if the groundwork has been properly laid. In those situations in which a customer is not quite ready to purchase, or has a concern that is getting in the way of the purchase, a different tact is necessary.

All too often, the objections and doubts that arise prevent the timid artist or gallerist from ever asking for the close; it is as though the salesperson would rather not make the sale than to have to deal with an objection. Looking at the sale this way is upside down. It is essential to know the client's concerns if they are to be addressed and allayed. The process does require a bit of finesse, along with a dab of courage, and a smattering of confidence.

Let us begin the challenge of helping your customer to resolve his concerns by listing the most common objections that arise in the close of a sale:

- I need to think about it.

- We just started looking and we want to see what else is out there.

- It might not be the right size.

- It's too big.

- It's too small.

- We don't have any more room for art.

- Our house won't be finished for six months.

You are cringing even as you read these objections because you've heard them all time and time again. But just because an objection has been raised, the possibility of a sale need not evaporate.

Don't give up – get to work!

Restate the Client's Concern

Your immediate reaction to an objection may be to offer a resolution. Though you will certainly be working to help the client help himself to resolve his concern, it is not your place to dive right in with the solution. Take a moment to restate the concern in your own words.

Even if the concern seems perfectly straight forward, this activity serves a dual purpose. First, it reassures the client you are listening, and that you have his best interest at heart. Second, by restating the dilemma, you are actually priming the customer to solve his own problem. When you allow him to find his way around the obstacle, you empower him to make the purchase through the strength of his own agency and will.

"I need to think about it," a client says.

"You need time to consider whether the piece is right for you?" I ask.

"I don't have a single square inch of wall space left in my home," a client states emphatically.

"And so you are in a tough spot, because even if you absolutely fall in love with this piece, you don't have any wall space left to display it if you acquire it?"

Remember, you are not asking these questions cold turkey; you have already begun the process of building a relationship with the customer. Be considerate and refrain from restating the hindrance sarcastically or incredulously.

Having given expression to your take on the situation, now give the customer an opportunity to affirm and to elaborate. He will often disclose additional information. He might even minimize the concern upon hearing you rephrase it, realizing that it is not necessarily insurmountable.

Make a subtle shift away from the dirth of available space, and emphasize how much he loves the artwork. Offer to take the item to his home to assist him in finding the perfect placement. With patience and the appropriate strategy, most obstructions can be overcome.

Uncover the True Concern by Asking Questions: Perfecting the Strategy

Getting to the heart of a client's concerns often requires a detective's skill. She can't always be relied upon to express her reservations; or as one of my favorite television characters, Dr. Gregory House is fond of saying: "People lie."

It is not that her intent is to deceive. For her own reasons, she finds it less complicated to give an excuse than to disclose her real reason for not purchasing. Here, as in many situations previously illustrated, asking the strategic questions will enable the experienced salesperson to discover the source of her reluctance.

The initial concern has been established, and she is now given the opportunity to elaborate. An effective question at this juncture might be:

"Is there anything else?"

Through this interrogative, she is invited to articulate, and to define the boundaries of her apprehension. The essence of the query is:

"So if we remove this stumbling block, there's nothing else in the way of your decision to purchase the piece?"

The probes will now be based upon the particular stumbling block that impedes the path to the sale. Let's look at some specific follow up questions for specific blocks:

"I need to think about it," the customer responds to your attempt to close.

"Certainly. This is an important piece of art, and you feel like you need some time to consider whether the piece is right?"

"Yes."

"Tell me about your process for determining whether a piece is right for you."

The response to this request will obviously vary with each shopper. What will remain a constant in every negotiation will be the delivery of insights for your use in propelling the customer toward the sale.

Let's take our previous scenario a bit further down the path:

"I am afraid we just don't have any more space in our house."

"And so you are in a tough spot. Even if you are completely enchanted with this piece, you don't have any wall space left to display it if you acquire it?"

"Well, since we truly do love the piece, I suppose if push comes to shove, we can always figure out how where to find a spot for it. Perhaps we could consider replacing one of our older pieces."

"Which piece have you been thinking about changing?"

Once again, the aim is to engage the customer's mind in the pursuit of solving her own problem. The input from the salesperson must be phrased in such a way as to keep the focus on point.

I have sold art to people who have claimed they had no more space – it does happen. They usually joke about how they cannot believe they are doing this, as they hand over the credit card. I have also had clients who, upon further reflection, admit that it is not so much a matter of space, as it is a matter of how much they like the piece, or a worry that the price is too dear for their budget.

Terrific! These are issues that can also be addressed, and now that I know the actual drawbacks, I can do what it takes to overcome them. Bring it on!

Go the Extra Mile in Assisting the Buyer to Find Solutions

The obstacle to the sale has been uncovered. Boundaries have been delineated. Insights have been shared.

Are you ready to put your full effort into helping your customer solve his own problem? Can you put your trust in this approach, though it may seem counter-intuitive? Are you prepared to put aside your natural inclination to provide the solution?

You are confident you have the answer, and it would be so wonderful to cut to the chase by blurting out the "sensible thing to do". But hey, the guy is going to be far more confident in his decision to buy when he believes it to be his own decision. His degree of satisfaction will be commensurate with his presumed autonomy in the proceedings.

"You have indicated your doubt at having a place to hang the painting. How can I help you find a spot for it?"

"Well, I suppose we could make a sketch of the wall showing the existing arrangement, and determine whether this painting would fit in the display."

"Do you have the dimensions of the wall and the sizes of the existing paintings for our sketch?"

"Not with me, no. Would it be possible to take the painting to my home to have a look-see? I really need to try it in the space before I make a final decision."

"That's a great suggestion. Since you are seriously interested, I would be happy to allow you to try it out in your home. How can I make that happen for you?"

"I live across town. Could we arrange to have it delivered?" or "I live out of state. Is there any chance we could have it shipped?"

- *Arrange for the Client to See the Artwork in His Home*

Notice I didn't simply offer to deliver the piece to his home; I let him make the suggestion that it be delivered or shipped. He came up with the "sensible action" to remedy his own dilemma.

- *Offer to Reframe the Artwork*

If the client has expressed concern about the frame of the painting not working with his décor, I ask him what frame he imagines would work best. I then inform him I am happy to reframe the painting to satisfy his preference, and ask about a convenient time to meet at the frame shop to look at new moldings.

The greater his investment in creative sensibility, time, and effort, the greater his determination will be to make the art his own. Engage him in the process.

- *Create a Sense of Urgency*

Occasionally a client expresses the concern that she has "only begun looking at art", and wants to look around some more before committing to a particular piece. That's perfectly understandable. Nevertheless, she must be informed that though you do have her best interest at heart, you would hate to see her miss out on the piece should someone else decide to buy it.

"I can see how much you like this painting – what would happen if you decided it was perfect for you, only to come back and find it had been sold to someone else?"

At a recent ArtWalk (the Scottsdale gallery district where my gallery is located holds one every Thursday evening), one of my staff had a couple come into the gallery early in the evening and fall in love with a particular piece of art. My salesperson did everything correctly in moving the clients to a commitment, but they had just started their stroll through the galleries and wanted to look around before they made a decision.

A little later in the evening, another couple came into the gallery and purchased the very piece the first couple had been considering. Here we have a gallery with hundreds of items on display, and this second couple comes in and purchases the work in which the first couple had expressed interest. What are the chances? One would think they would be pretty low, but such things do happen. Call it karma or the alignment of the planets, but it often seems a particular piece of artwork suddenly becomes a hot commodity.

One can only imagine how devastated the first couple was when they came back to the gallery and learned the piece they had now decided to purchase was sold. We were fortunate (or skilled) enough to be able to help the couple choose another item. Even so, they left a little less happy than they would have, had they purchased their first choice when they first saw it.

I share this story with collectors who are sitting on the fence, trying to decide whether they should act now. At the conclusion of the tale of woe, I inquire: "How would you feel if the same thing happened with this piece?"

I encourage them to think about their affinity for the work, and raise the specter of the possibility of their missing out on the chance to own it. While I'd never wish to be called a fear monger, I have learned that fear is one of the few emotions that encourages immediate action.

Of course the collectors might say, "We will survive if it sells," and choose not to act. I would rather risk this reaction and force the issue, than not ask, only to lose the sale anyway. Remember, once they walk out the door, the chance of making the sale decreases dramatically – almost to zero.

Don't Try to Solve Problems Before You Know They Exist

Salespeople are sometimes tempted to deal with doubts and concerns before they actually arise. This is especially true of gallerists and artists who participate in frequent shows. After a while, they begin to recognize patterns in the doubts so frequently expressed to them, and to hear those same doubts echoed in their dreams: "I need to think about it," "I need to show my husband," or "I don't have any more space for art."

A natural inclination is to offer solutions to these and other concerns before they are ever voiced; a sort of preemptive strike before she can put up a fight. It might seem a clever strategy to offer each browser the option to take the artwork out on approval as soon as she pauses in front of a painting. It could appear as advantageous to offer photos and brochures of a sculpture as soon as someone glances at it. Unfortunately, there is a serious flaw in this approach to "head 'er off at the pass": the salesperson is, once again, trying to solve the problem, rather than assisting the customer to solve the problem (be it real or imagined) herself.

To reiterate: You will be most effective in making sales if you put every effort into helping your customers resolve their own concerns.

The intent is to sell the artwork now. Offering solutions preemptively may derail the desired result to close the sale today. (See Chapter 7 | Go for the Close to understand the dangers of false closings.)

CHAPTER 9 | NEGOTIATE!

"Is that your best price?"

Many salespeople and artists quiver at the very sound of the words – I relish them, and all that they portend.

If a client is at the point where he is asking about price, one can assume he is primed and prepared to buy. When the subject of price comes up, it's a good time to rejoice, because all other potential concerns related to a sale are now off the table. The client is in effect saying, "I like the piece. I want to buy it. If we can come to an agreement on price, I will buy it."

I can't imagine a more promising declaration! Though I enjoy the negotiation process, I have found that I am the rare exception. Some salespeople dread the very thought of negotiation. Many artists are actually offended when a potential buyer makes an offer other than the sticker price. It is the general consensus that life would be much easier if customers would simply agree to pay full price for every item.

I am a realist and a pragmatist. Because I live in the real world, and the world as I experience it is a world where customers are apt to ask for discounts, I've made up my mind to be the superlative negotiator. More clients are now asking for discounts than when I started in the business. This might be both a reflection of changing economic times, and an indication that buyers are becoming savvier when it comes to purchasing art.

My regular clients can well afford to pay full price if they wish. I suspect it's rarely a matter of their having an issue with the price; they frankly want to feel that they have gotten a good deal. They, too, as often as not, enjoy the give and take afforded by a lively negotiation.

The majority of my clients are successful in business, and are thus adept at negotiating deals and proposals – it would be ridiculous to assume they would not bring the same skills to buying art. If I were unwilling to negotiate, I would squander one of the most powerful tools in my sales tool chest, and drastically limit my ability to close sales. Why would I want to put myself at an unnecessary disadvantage?

I am not sure how negotiating got a bad name - haggling used to be the standard procedure in every transaction, and in much of the world it still is. Prices need not be viewed as though they were written in blood!

I recently made a sale to a collector who related his experience with another gallery on the street. He had been interested in purchasing a particular painting, and had made an offer (a reasonable offer, in his estimation). The salesperson informed him that the gallery did not discount artwork – no exceptions.

The collector left the gallery without a backward glance, and is unlikely to return. He has since purchased a tremendous number of items from our gallery, and has always proved to be reasonable in our transactions. I am sure the gallery he visited had its reasons not to negotiate, but it seems to me it is doing itself, its artists, and its clientele a disservice with its rigid policy of no negotiation. In today's economic environment, the necessity to negotiate is a given.

When Pricing Your Artwork, Build in Room to Negotiate

With the knowledge that negotiation is likely to occur, it makes sound sense to account for it when setting prices. In my first book, *"Starving" to Successful,* I devote an entire chapter to the mechanics of determining the pricing of one's work. While it is not my purpose to cover the details for price setting here, I do encourage the artist and the gallerist to build in some room to negotiate when pricing art. The breadth of each negotiation will vary, but if one allows a 20% margin for negotiation, she will have sufficient flexibility for virtually every scenario.

An artist selling her work directly to collectors at shows and through her studio, while also showing in galleries, needs to make sure she is pricing her work consistently. Her galleries need to have the same latitude to negotiate with customers that she adopts when making direct sales. The 20% margin must therefore be the standard application across the board.

Get the Client to Make an Offer

When a client approaches me inquiring whether the price of a particular piece is negotiable, I reply that the artist does give me a little bit of room to move if it will help a client who loves the piece to acquire it. I then state the retail price on the piece, and ask what the client has in mind. It is my strong preference to have the client put a number on the table before I start fishing for an alternate price.

What if the customer makes a ridiculously low offer? I don't let it phase me, and I take no offense. After all, the initial offer is not the end of the negotiation process; it is just the beginning.

Not every client will be willing to put a specific offer on the table – "I just want your very best price," is a common declaration. I don't push hard to get a number, but if I can get the customer to make an offer, I have found it makes the rest of the negotiation progress more smoothly.

I have also discovered that the typical collector will not low-ball me with a ludicrous offer. By requesting that he make an offer, I am putting him ever so gently on the spot. While he wants a great bargain on the art, he neither wants to embarrass himself, nor to offend me. Occasionally, the first offer from the customer entails the need for a smaller discount than I would have proffered.

Confirm the Offer and Commit the Customer

As soon as the client has given me a number, I echo the offer. Then I get a firm commitment that if I find a way to make the offer work, the transaction will be completed today.

"You are offering $4,500 – if I can make that number work, will you purchase the sculpture today?"

Requiring the client to commit in the here-and-now eliminates the opportunity to introduce other obstacles that might compromise the purchase. I don't want to begin intense negotiations if he still needs to measure a space, or to decide if he likes the sculpture enough to secure it – I will negotiate only if he is ready to purchase at the mutually acceptable price.

Write Up a Counter-Offer

Now that the client has committed to purchase the piece, I ask for a moment. I make my way back to my desk, where I enter a state of intense calculation. I am going to admit it: I put on a bit of a show here. Even though I usually know what my counter-offer is going to be as soon as the client has made her offer, I never (NEVER!) accept nor counter an offer straightway.

I sit at my desk and calculate. I pull up my inventory database and confirm the retail price. I pull out a notepad and jot down figures. I run the numbers on my calculator. I calculate, I contemplate, all the while scratching numbers on my notepad (more about what I write on the pad to come). I furrow my brow and mutter under my breath.

Why all the fuss? There is a method in my madness: I want the client to know I am working hard for him – and I am.

At the conclusion of all the calculation and contemplation, I finally reach the moment of triumph – the moment wherein I have figured out how to make my clients the proud owners of a new work of art, at an incredible value.

During this three-minute exercise in "crunching the numbers", my anxious patrons have either been making their way around the gallery, or waiting before the piece of art for my answer. They can't help but make furtive glances in my direction, and take notice of the intensity in my application. There are moments when they think I will surely come back with bad news, perhaps even chase them out of the gallery for making such a preposterous offer.

Now, at the triumphal moment, an exultant smile has taken over my face. It becomes clear that everything is going to be okay. I rise from my chair, and stride briskly to where they stand to deliver the happy news.

On my notepad, I have written the following:

$5,000.00 Retail $4700 All-inclusive

+$180.00 Delivery/Shipping

$5,180.00

  +$82.50 Sales Tax

$5,262.50 Total

I have purposefully made the left column to appear complex and expensive, in sharp contrast to the beautiful simplicity of the right column. I use my notepad to illustrate the counter-offer.

"I think I have come up with something that will work for you," I say. "Let me show you what I was able to do."

When I extend the pad for their examination, I initially cover my counter-offer with my right thumb. I proceed to explain, step-by-step, the retail price and any additional charges. I conclude by underlining the retail price.

"The retail on this piece is $5,000. I estimate the crating and delivery would be about $180, which brings us to $5,180. Because we're shipping out of state, there is no state sales tax;

however, there is an $82.50 charge to satisfy the city tax. That brings the total to five thousand, two hundred sixty-two dollars, and fifty cents."

I want that last number to be long, complex, and expensive. I give the full version instead of shortening it to fifty-two, sixty-two, and fifty cents ($5,262.50).

"It is my pleasure to offer the piece to you at $4,700 (and I say it forty-seven hundred, not four thousand, seven hundred) all-inclusive. I will cover the tax and the delivery."

I skip a couple of beats while they look at the pad, and then I move to close.

"May I write that up for you?"

Many times, the couple in this position sees and acknowledges everything that I am doing for them, nods, and accepts the deal at $4,700. We move to the desk to write up the sale (see Chapter 7 | Go for the Close).

There are, however, many instances when the clients look at the counter offer, and then make a counter-counter offer. In this example, it might be $4,500.

"$4,500?" I restate. "And you would have me include the shipping and tax?"

Upon confirmation from the clients that I understand their counter offer correctly, I pause for another moment, and then extend my hand to shake theirs and say, "It would be my pleasure. Congratulations – the piece is yours."

Notice that I did not say anything about the couple's original offer during the negotiation. The initial offer may have been $4,500, but remember, I was using that offer to ascertain where the client stood, and to make sure I did not offer a deeper discount than was sought or expected. The original offer may have had some impact on the size of the discount, but had it been absurdly low, it would in no way have dictated my response.

Never Apologize When Presenting the Counter-Offer

I remember very early in my sales career hearing a colleague return to a customer who had made an offer and say something to the effect:

"I'm sorry, but it looks like the best I can do is . . ."

Think about this response for a minute. What he was saying to his customer translated as: "Prepare yourself to be disappointed and to not buy." Even then, with very little training or experience, I knew that this was not the message I wanted to convey in my own transactions.

I understand the inclination to say something like what I overheard, especially in the situation where my number differs radically from the offer. My approach, though, is to simply pretend the low offer does not exist – it was never made. I return to the customer, proud to share the great value I have secured for them.

"I think I've come up with something that is going to work for you. Let me show you what I have done."

Now, instead of priming the customer for disappointment, I have secured his readiness to hear the great news I have in hand. I show him my notepad, covering my counter-offer with my thumb. I emphasize the expensive retail price first, and then finish on a high note when I uncover the magic number in the right column.

Make Someone Else the Bad Guy

This advice won't work for the artist. After all, when it comes to her work, the buck stops with her. For gallerists (or artists' spouses), moving the decision making process away from oneself can be an excellent way to conduct a negotiation.

"I need to make a quick phone call and check with the artist – can you give me just a moment?"

I love saying this to the customer. As soon as I say the words, two things happen. First, I make the buyer an ally in the negotiation process. (Guess who just became the bad guy?) Second, he suddenly realizes he is transacting business not only with the gallery owner, but is also negotiating with the artist herself. This knowledge can maximize the client's offer.

If You Cannot Agree, Get Out Gracefully

In spite of your best efforts, you will occasionally experience negotiations that hold no possibility for successful resolution or positive outcome. A customer might be unwilling or unable to pay enough to make the transaction profitable for you. When this is the case, maintain your cool, and be gracious in declining his offer. Make the attempt to leave the door open should he have a change of heart upon further reflection.

"Thank you for your offer. Unfortunately I am unable to accept it at this time. My offer of $4,500 remains open to you if you change your mind, so long as the piece is still available."

Notice I do not offer a reason why I cannot accept the offer (more on that to come), nor do I tell the customer to take a hike. I remain professional, yet make it clear that I have gone as low as I can go. Perhaps the customer will step back to confer with a companion, or to give my offer further consideration, before agreeing to accept the terms. But even if he decides to walk away, he can now do so with the assurance that I have respected him and his offer, and have treated him fairly and squarely.

Never Argue with nor Try to Explain
Your Pricing to Your Customer

I have observed artists entering protracted discussions with potential clients, going to great lengths to explain why they cannot accept an offer. Their reasons might include: the time that goes into each piece; the cost of the materials; the skilled techniques involved; the intensive labor brought to bear; the importance of maintaining the integrity and intrinsic value of the artwork. All valid reasons, clearly, but of no consequence whatsoever to the uninitiated browser.

Worse yet, too many artists lecture the would-be-buyer, or argue with him about the price. Nothing good is ever going to result from an argument with a customer. It is difficult enough to reason someone to a price; he will never be argued or bullied there. The sale is lost at the outset of the rant. A doomed sale. An offended shopper. A sorry scene. An unpleasant afternoon, indeed.

Word-of-mouth is a double edged sword. The last thing an artist needs is to have his reputation besmirched by an irate collector on the loose, with an axe to grind.

To the Gallery Owner

Empower your salespeople by giving them the power to negotiate. While ultimate authority for sales and discounts rests with you, giving your salespeople the latitude to negotiate will allow them to close sales you might miss out on when you are not available to manage the negotiations.

Do set parameters for the negotiation. "You may not discount deeper than 15% without talking to me," for example.

Train your staff in negotiation stratagem to enable them to bargain effectively for you.

This approach will prove itself in escalating sales. Use your team. Trust in their competence.

CHAPTER 10 | WHEN ALL ELSE FAILS, FOLLOW UP

As has been established in earlier chapters, there will be times when you are unable to close the sale on the spot, despite your impressive expertise. Even if you do everything right, there is no guarantee of success, written or otherwise. Clearly, in the best of worlds, business is concluded on the initial visit – you are happy, the collector is happy, and everyone can breathe a sigh of relief.

But what if all does not go as planned? What then?

In the case of the runaway shopper, you ought to have a system of operation in place that addresses the practice of follow up. But for follow up, each and every "unclosed sale" that walks out your door is lost forever.

The follow up requires care, continuity, and consistency. Be careful not to irritate your customer with incessant communication. Do only as much follow up as is reasonable to prevent the lead from growing cold. Continue to exude cheerful optimism and good will with each contact.

It is ultimately too little contact that dooms the potential for a sale. I have found that it generally requires seven to ten follow up communications to close a deal. Giving up after the first or second attempt demonstrates a defeatist policy unworthy of the master sales guru.

In the next pages, I will share an outline of my follow up regimen, which you can then adapt to your particular situation and requirement. While I follow the basic format, I do customize each communication to the client, referencing our earlier encounter and our previous conversation. I want each contact I make to feel unique and personal.

Gather Contact Information

I am far more interested in getting my customer's follow up information than I am in giving him a brochure or business card, and then hoping for the best. Giving out a brochure or business card is a last resort – this happens only after I have successfully obtained his contact information, or have been rebuffed in every attempt to do so.

You are going to have a hard time following up if you don't manage to collect your client's contact information. Gaining access to this information requires skill. It is a vital precursor to the line-up of steps leading to the deferred sale. Instead of requesting his credit card for an immediate closure, you are requesting his private, personal, and precious contact data as the means whereby you can stay in touch.

To reiterate: Do not seek this information until all other attempts to sell have failed. Because it is easier to gather contact information than it is to close a sale, you may be incentivized to extract the address early in an encounter. However, when you let the ease of collecting an email address tempt you to focus your sales efforts here instead of where they should be - on making the sale - you are writing your own license to fail. RESIST THIS TEMPTATION!

The ideal way to get a client's contact information is to write it on a sales slip as he is handing over his credit card. Always put your energy into making things happen to fit the ideal; don't make the drill more difficult than it has to be by delaying the sale.

Now that we have that out of the way, let me share a few of my secrets for acquiring contact information. Though it is indeed easier than making a sale, it does demand a bit of finesse.

People are understandably reluctant to share their phone numbers, both land and cell, and their addresses, both snail mail and email. We live in an age in which we are bombarded with advertisements, solicitations, and notices – JUNK. No one is excited about the prospect of receiving additional unsolicited calls and mailings.

Fortunately, when you've done a good job of laying the foundation for a relationship, your client will trust you not to misuse his information. You can commiserate about overloaded inboxes and intrusive phone calls.

"Oh, that we could escape the deluge! I can't blame you for wanting to restrict additional access to your inbox and mailbox and phone lines!"

With all of this in mind, give careful consideration to how you ask for the address.

Asking outright, "May I have your contact information?" is likely to push a person into automatic defense mode. He will surely bristle at the suggestion that he should be expected to summarily surrender his privacy.

Try instead, "Would you like me to email you an image of this piece? I can include the dimensions and additional detail for you."

Better yet, take an assumptive approach. In my gallery, I have client contact cards secured on small clipboards. When a customer prepares to leave the gallery, I extend a clipboard and a pen and say, "I will email you an image of the piece along with dimensions, pricing, and additional detail." Make this a cheery, breezy overture, and watch it work like a charm.

People have a tendency to be equable, and to follow the path of least resistance. The best part about getting the client to fill out the contact form instead of directly asking for the information is that he will indubitably fill out the entire form, giving not only an email address, but a physical address and phone numbers as well.

Now, to make good on the promise of an effectual paradigm for following through on the follow up.

Follow Up #1 | Immediately After the Encounter | Thank the Customer and Provide Information.

My first follow up typically occurs immediately after my interaction with the customer. I sit down at my computer and compose an email while our meeting is fresh in my mind. Often, the customer receives the message in his inbox (or on his Smartphone) before he is down the block.

A typical email reads something like this:

Dear Jim and Kathy,

Thank you for visiting Xanadu Gallery this afternoon. It was a pleasure getting to know you and discussing Robert Burt's artwork. "Sunday Drive" is a great piece and I can tell how much you both love it. As promised, I am including a photo of the piece below, along with the dimensions and a brief biography of the artist.

I know this piece would make a treasured addition to your collection. Please let me know how I may be of service in helping you acquire this piece.

Sincerely,

Jason

J. Jason Horejs

Xanadu Gallery

I include a digital image of the artwork, either directly in the email or as an attachment.

I always make sure to test my emails to ensure that images are coming through with the email. This can be (as anyone knows) trickier than anticipated. I know it's got to be tricky because I often receive messages from artists who think they have included an image, when all I see is an empty box, or an unopenable attachment.

Unfortunately, I cannot disclose a list of failsafe steps to make certain that the images are coming through, as the list will vary with individual operating systems and email carriers. I can, however, recommend that an artist or gallerist send tests to friends on Macs and PCs, and then confirm that they are able to open the email and view the images, and that the format of the email is easy to read and looks good.

When one runs into problems, the internet is replete with helpful forums that dispense assistance in correcting settings and maximizing operative effectiveness. Assistance is always as close as your keyboard and your computer screen.

Follow Up #2 | Four Days After Initial Contact | Thank-You and Confirmation of First Email

Often, the first email will fail to elicit any response, or may get only a brief acknowledgement. That's okay – I merely want my client to see how efficient I am, and how sincere I am in my commitment to provide superior service.

My next email is intended to elicit a response and to initiate a renewed dialogue.

Dear Jim and Kathy,

Thank you again for visiting Xanadu while in Scottsdale. I hope you enjoyed the rest of your stay and had an uneventful trip home to Minneapolis.

As promised, I sent you an image of "Sunday Drive" by Robert Burt, along with dimensions, and some information about the artist.

What have you been thinking about the piece? How will the piece look in your room?

I emailed the artist and asked if he had any additional details he would like to share about the piece, and I thought you might find his comments about the piece interesting. I have included his email below.

I am looking forward to hearing back from you, and being of assistance in helping you add this amazing painting to your collection.

Sincerely,

Jason

J. Jason Horejs

Xanadu Gallery

Notice everything I am attempting to do here. First and foremost, I am keeping the communication as personal as possible. The last thing I want is for this letter to feel like it is a cut-and-paste form letter. Hence the use of first names and the reference to the trip back home.

In the second paragraph, I am working to establish a sense of obligation and connection between us. I am delivering on my half of the contract by fulfilling my promise to communicate, with the expectation that "Jim and Kathy" will pay me the courtesy of a response.

In paragraph three, I have let the customers know I am going the extra mile to provide additional, valuable information. I am putting time and effort toward helping them make the decision, rather than waiting around for them to send me a check.

Asking the artist to write a few words about the piece is great not only for the client, but for me and the artist as well. It provides me with additional information about the piece that I would not otherwise have, and gives me an opportunity to alert the artist that I have someone interested in his work. I am careful when doing this not to build expectations too high. On the one hand, I don't want my artist disappointed if the sale doesn't ultimately close, but on the other, I generally find that he is thrilled to be told there is interest in and activity on his work. In his desire to be accommodating, he is more than happy to give me a few words.

To be honest, I occasionally do a bit of editing upon receipt of an artist's response. When I have it tweaked, I put the information on file, along with the image, so I can readily access it when I have someone else interested in the same piece.

In the event the artist is acting as salesperson for her own work, she has undoubtedly already informed the interested party concerning the background of the piece, and likely has nothing new to share. That's okay; she need only remind him in writing what she shared when he was visiting. It will heighten the significance of the artwork in his estimation when he reads the words of the artist, detailing her own work. A response from him is typical for this second email.

Follow Up #3 | Four Days After Initial Contact | Mail a Letter and Printed Picture of the Piece

If I have a physical address for the client, the same day I am sending email #2, I will also send out a letter via the good-old-fashioned post office. This letter is hand-written and handstamped. Though it is going to mirror much of what I have already said in my emails, I want to hit them on every possible front. Getting something tangible and tactile into their hands will sometimes work when an email won't.

Dear Jim and Kathy,

Thank you again for visiting Xanadu and for your interest in "Sunday Drive" by Robert Burt. I have sent you several email images of the piece, but I thought it might be helpful to have a photo for your reference and for your files once you have the piece.

I am looking forward to hearing back from you. Please let me know if I may provide any additional information.

Sincerely,

Jason

J. Jason Horejs

Xanadu Gallery

I often include a printed copy of the artist's bio in this letter, as well as anything I have from the artist that references this particular piece. The weight of the additional detail tends to further stimulate an interest in what is perceived to be a significant work of art.

Follow Up #4 | Phone Call | Seven Days After Initial Contact

If Jim and Kathy have provided a phone number, don't hesitate to pick up the phone and call them when a week has passed since the initial contact. Make the call pleasant, brief, and friendly.

"Mr. Smith, this is Jason from Xanadu Gallery in Scottsdale, AZ - how are you, sir?"

"Fine, Jason," Mr. Smith responds, "How are you?"

"I'm very well, thank you. I am calling to confirm you received my emails regarding 'Sunday Drive' by Robert Burt."

The customer, in all likelihood, says thanks for the email and offers an excuse as to why he hasn't gotten back to you.

"That's no problem – I can imagine how busy you are. I look at the piece every day in the gallery, and I remember how much you and Kathy enjoyed it. I just want to make sure you have all the information you need to acquire the piece."

The phone call gives the salesperson the advantage of being able to ask fundamental questions, to follow up with specific questions, and to utilize the client's answers to uncover his concerns. With this information, the artist or gallerist is better able to allay Mr. Smith's reservations.

Follow Up #5 | Nine Days After Initial Contact

The further one gets into the follow up process, the more difficult it becomes to adhere to a set pattern. Much of the activity will now be dictated by the knowledge derived from the clients' responses to the first couple of emails. As the process progresses, the communication should grow more personal. In essence, the attempt now becomes that of re-creating, then building upon, the original face-to-face overtures to close the sale. The channels of email, snail mail, and telephone must now suffice as the only means to make contact with Jim and Kathy.

If I am not getting much response from the buyer, my general strategy is to reiterate points I have made in previous communications, through the retelling of the story that accompanies the art. I provide supplementary tidbits of biographical information about the artist. I sprinkle in details about the positive response Jim and Kathy expressed when they saw the art for the first time. The goal continues to be to engage the clients in the conversation, and to evoke a response.

These communications (typically emails) are going to be brief but personal. I don't mind if Jim and Kathy start to feel like they owe me some kind of reply for all my efforts – there really is a method to my madness!

Each subsequent email includes a digital image of the piece, and relays another detail of interest.

Dear Jim & Kathy,

Just a quick follow up on my notes from last week. Have you had a chance to further review the images, and consider the art for your space? What additional questions do you have regarding the piece?

I was reminded of a brief article published in a local art publication regarding the artist and his work. I thought you might enjoy reading it, and have provided an excerpt below.

Please let me know how I may be of service,

Jason

J. Jason Horejs

Xanadu Gallery

While I sincerely do want to continue to provide useful information to the collectors, my communication has now effectively become a battle of attrition. If I manage to keep the emails and letters buzzing, eventually Jim and Kathy are going to wear down and respond, even if their response is only to tell me to knock it off because they are no longer interested.

A common concern among both gallery staff and artist is a fear that if they keep trying, they run the risk of irritating their customers. I have never found this to be the case, and even if it were to happen, I would prefer to risk upsetting a customer than to risk the possibility of not making a sale. If I do not orchestrate a persistent follow up, I do not close a sale. It is that simple.

Remember, customers are busy with work, family and life. Even when they mean to respond, they sometimes don't because life gets in the way. Jim and Kathy deserve my best follow up enterprise.

Simply put, I would rather receive the irritated email asking me to stop, than to give up, never knowing whether I could have made the sale had I persisted a bit longer. I am doing a good thing when I strive to facilitate the collectors' desire to procure a wonderful work of art. I have no reason to apologize, and no cause to be ashamed.

Follow Up #6 | 14 Days After First Contact

If I have not received any communications after a couple of weeks, it is time to start digging a little deeper and pulling out some bigger emotional artillery. I will now dig for guilt if I have to (though I will do so with subtlety) and I will start taking some measured risks to elicit a reaction.

Dear Jim & Kathy,

It has been several weeks since we met and you saw Robert Burt's piece, "Sunday Drive". I have provided the details and images I promised. Please let me know if I have failed to provide any information you need to help you acquire the piece.

I sensed you both loved the art, and I want to make sure I am not failing in any way to render the service necessary to your success.

I look forward to hearing back from you soon!

Jason

J. Jason Horejs

Xanadu Gallery

Follow Up #7 | 21 Days after First Contact

At three weeks out, I pull out all the stops and rush in headlong to win the customers' attention. I make an offer I have held in reserve prior to this point in time.

Dear Jim & Kathy,

I would like to make you an offer I think you will have a hard time refusing. I keep thinking back to our conversation about "Sunday Drive" by Robert Burt and how perfect you thought it would be in your home.

I have found there are times when you simply cannot know how well a piece will fit in your space, and in your life, until you see it there in person.

I often allow my clients to view a piece of artwork in their homes with no commitment or obligation on their parts.

It would be my pleasure to have the piece crated and delivered to your home, where you could live with it for a week.

You have nothing to lose. Should you decide the piece simply doesn't work, just let me know and I will make arrangements to have the piece returned. I will pay shipping both directions.

Please email or call at your earliest convenience and I will make the necessary arrangements.

Best Regards,

Jason

As I said, I do not make this offer up front – it could delay a sale. Some customers will respond to the first or second communication (this would be ideal of course), and decide to buy the piece. I wouldn't want to delay that purchase by offering to send the piece out on approval before the 7th email.

At this point, however, it's time to make something happen. By offering to pay for the shipping in both directions, I have removed any risk for the collectors to try the piece. I have found there is typically little risk involved for us, as most clients who are willing to have the piece shipped to them are also likely to purchase.

When to Give Up

What if I don't make the sale after the seventh contact - should I give up? No!

Even if the client hasn't yet been willing to commit to the purchase, the possibility of the sale somewhere down the road still exists. Continued follow up requires some effort, but because the possible benefit so far outweighs the cost, it just makes sense to practice persistence.

I have had many cases in which a sale came months down the road, and only after many, many contacts. As I write this book, I am working on a sale that began over nine months ago.

The clients found a piece in the gallery they felt would be perfect for a new sunroom addition to their home. At the time of their first visit to the gallery, they were in the midst of remodeling and weren't (in spite of my best salesmanship) ready to make a commitment.

I promptly initiated my follow up process, knowing that it was likely to take some time to put the sale together. After an initial response, the clients went silent. I made a reminder to myself to follow up down the road. Six months after our meeting, I sent another email and got a response from the wife that they were actually nearing the end of their reconstruction project, but had run into some unexpected expenses. However, they remembered the piece, and requested that I check back again in several months.

Of course I did check back, and we are now actively negotiating to close the sale. In our most recent series of communications, I rolled out the full presentation, and included a note from the artist wherein he again expressed his enthusiasm about the piece.

I cannot be certain the sale will close successfully, but I can be certain that had I given up after our first round of correspondence, I would never have had the opportunity to re-open the conversation and have a shot at the close.

I remember an instance several years ago in which I closed a sale only after several dozen communiqués, stretched over the period of six months! In that instance, it truly was a matter of patiently persisting until the time was right for the customer.

Craft and implement a follow up system that will enable you to keep your efforts organized and consistent. While we presently keep track of our clients in a computer database, perhaps it would make more sense for someone else to use a manual system to organize his client list, similar to the one we used when we first opened the gallery.

In that system, we used the address card (see Chapter 3 | What's in a Name?) to record a client's information, and then moved the card through a series of folders as we followed up. For example, every Monday we went through the files and looked at everyone's cards, and followed up with whichever step corresponded to his placement order in the folders. Each client would get a note, email, or phone call, after which his card would be transferred into the next file, where it would be handy for the next step in follow up. It was customary to jot a note on the back of the card regarding the follow up and any response we received.

Come up with a system that works, and then stick with it. Follow up consistently and persistently, and your sales will increase. Guaranteed!

(Of course, a side benefit of all of this following up is that your client is going to have a hard time forgetting who you are. Even if he does not purchase now, he will think of you the next time he considers adding to his collection.)

Keep Evolving Your Follow Up Protocol

I consider this chapter a work in progress. Simply put, this is my current follow up system; ask me again in a year's time, and the notes and follow up protocol will have further evolved.

In writing notes and following up consistently, you will find your own voice and develop the system that works best for you. I encourage you, no matter what the system is, to strive to be consistent and persistent in your follow up with each and every client.

CHAPTER 11 | TURN CLIENTS INTO COLLECTORS

Making a sale to a client is a rewarding and gratifying experience, but if that is the end of one's interaction, he is missing out on an opportunity to build a profitable and enjoyable long-term relationship.

When someone has made a major purchase, she has demonstrated she trusts the salesperson and has given a clear indication of interest in a unique body of work. Capitalize on her professional trust by going the extra mile to cultivate an ongoing relationship.

Send a Thank You Note

Make it a habit to send a hand-written thank you note to buyers as soon as possible after completing the sale and delivering the artwork. If a person has walked away with the artwork, sit down and promptly write the note. When the artwork is being delivered or shipped, wait until notification of its safe arrival before sending the note.

In the event we ship the artwork, we let the clients know once the piece has been crated and shipped, and include the tracking number. We then call or email again upon notification that the package has been received to make sure the art has arrived intact.

It would not be a good thing were a thank you note to arrive, in the event the precious cargo had been destroyed by our friends with the delivery company. Only after its safe arrival has been confirmed should the thank you missive be sent.

We have had custom cards with our logo printed, but thank you cards from an office supply store will be just as effective. The thank you card is an opportunity to both thank the customers, and compliment them once again upon their purchase. The sentiment should be short and simple.

> Dear Jim & Kathy,
>
> Thank you again for your purchase of "Sunday Drive." I appreciate your business, and enjoyed helping you bring this incredible piece into your collection. I know that you, your friends, and family members will enjoy the piece for many years to come.
>
> If there is ever any way I may be of service, please don't hesitate to contact me.
>
> Sincerely,
>
> Jason
>
> Jason Horejs
>
> Xanadu Gallery

Send a Thank You Gift

Several years ago, we implemented a 1% policy at the gallery. That is, for each purchase, we apply 1% of the sales amount toward the procurement of a thank you gift for our customer.

For a small purchase, 1% may do no more than cover the cost of the thank you card; but for larger dollar amounts, 1% will procure a bouquet of fresh flowers. With the highest dollar sales, we routinely send a small piece of art as a thank you gift.

These small investments pay large dividends in building long-term relationships with one's customers. Applying the Golden Rule in every aspect of every transaction with every buyer will spell success for the wise artist and for the sagacious gallerist.

Ask for a Testimonial

Four to six weeks after the sale is finalized, my gallery sends a post-sale survey to our customers. After thanking them again for their business, we ask them to respond to a series of questions about our mutual dealings, and about their satisfaction with the art now that it is in their home.

This survey is an opportunity for us to ascertain the levels of satisfaction with both the artwork and the service we provided. It is an effective means for us to elicit comments from the collector that will help us to make future sales.

Our survey queries are constantly changing and evolving, depending upon the sort of information we would like to emphasize and gather at a given point in time. Here is a sample of the questions we typically ask. Notice how we adhere to that mighty principle of asking open-ended questions, questions that lead to detailed responses, rather than to the brief and unproductive "yes" or "no" answers

---

Dear Jim and Kathy,

We want to take a moment to thank you again for your purchase of "Sunday Drive" by Robert Burt. Now that you have had several weeks to live with and enjoy the piece, would you please take a few moments and share your thoughts about the art, and give us some feedback regarding your experience purchasing from Xanadu?

This kind of feedback is invaluable to us in helping us to constantly improve our service to our clients. Additionally, if you will permit us to share your comments with our potential buyers, together we can assist them to feel confident and comfortable in acquiring art from our Xanadu artists.

The survey below should take no more than a few minutes to complete. You may simply hit reply to the email, and type your responses right into this email.

Thank you for your feedback, and as always, please let us know if there is any way we may be of service.

Jason

J. Jason Horejs

Xanadu Gallery

What impact has the artwork you purchased from Xanadu had upon your home?

What reaction has the art elicited from others who have seen it?

What is your favorite detail in the artwork?

How do you feel about the piece, now that you have had time to live with it?

How would you rate your experience purchasing from Xanadu?

Is there anything you perceive we could be doing to make the process simpler, and more enjoyable?

Do you have any other comments about the artwork, your purchase, or your experience?

May we share your comments with other collectors in our gallery, in our promotional materials, and on our website?

How would you like us to credit your comments? For example, we can simply list you as "Xanadu customer, Chicago, Illinois", or "Jim & Kathy B., Chicago Illinois", or we can list your full names and home town. We take your privacy seriously and will never share your personal or contact information with anyone.

Thank you for taking the time to complete this questionnaire. If you have a moment and could forward a photo of the piece in your home, we would love to see how it looks!

Correct Your Errors

Occasionally, something goes awry in the sales process. Artwork is damaged in shipping. A misunderstanding during negotiation leads to an incorrect charge. Lack of communication causes inconvenience for a customer.

The more people with whom one works, the more likely he is to run into a situation in which someone is dissatisfied with some detail of the transaction. Often, the dissatisfaction is no more than a minor inconvenience or small misunderstanding that can be readily corrected. At other times, however, major tension ensues.

It is best to look at a misapprehension as an avenue for the salesperson to impress the disgruntled buyer: His quick grasp of the situation, and his immediate action to remedy it, might well exceed the buyer's expectation for fair play.

"The customer is always right" mantra seems to have fallen out of favor as of late; but I am still a big believer in the philosophy behind the saying. When he loses in a dispute, ultimately, everyone loses. Dissatisfied, disgruntled, disaffected, disappointed. This guy will not only cease to buy your artwork, but he might become a source of negative advertising via word-of-mouth, as well.

Though correcting the problem with a customer could cost money, in the long-term, a difficulty well-handled is a sound investment in securing a future relationship. This would be an instance of the end justifying the means.

Several years ago, right around the time of the stock market crash in 2008, I had a client who ordered a sculpture from me. We didn't have the piece in the gallery, and the artist didn't have any castings of the sculpture available to ship, so we ordered a casting from the foundry.

Initially, we had quoted a "4-6 week" span of time for delivery of the new casting. Due to circumstances beyond our control, the shipment was delayed well beyond the anticipated date of arrival. It seemed as though everything that could go wrong did go wrong. Murphy's Law proved itself to be an apt adage.

Though the client was patient for a time, he eventually became irritated with the seemingly endless delays in getting the sculpture to him. Rather than try to excuse the delays, we kept the client informed of what was happening, and apologized profusely for the hold-up. When the sculpture finally arrived, we installed it with no charge to the customer.

It would have been easy to say, "Not our fault, just deal with it." Instead, we took full responsibility – to the point that we offered a refund on the customer's deposit should the delays continue much longer.

Our service-oriented approach proved to be successful not only in the completion of that sale, but in an additional sale as well. Several months ago, the same collector came back to the gallery for a show, and purchased another piece by the same artist. We saw this as a testament to the fact that we must have handled the situation correctly: a job well done.

If You Don't Have What Your Client Is Seeking, Help Him Find It

This may sound like sales suicide, but if a customer is looking for something in particular that you cannot provide, offer to help her find it elsewhere. If you have her best interest at heart, though you may not be able to sell to her today, when she sees your sincere desire to make her happy, you will have set the foundation for a life-long relationship.

My gallery often sends a customer to one of our competitors when we think another gallery might provide what our customer needs. This, of course, requires that we have some familiarity with what our various competitors are offering – a good idea anyway. We network with artists, visit galleries, and get to know the market.

We recently had a couple come into the gallery looking for a sculpture to give as a gift to their son and daughter-in-law for their 25th wedding anniversary. The parents had a very specific subject in mind – they were looking for two figures embracing, and they wanted a less contemporary, more traditional style. My gallery director, Elaine, showed them around the gallery and presented a couple of options. It soon became apparent that we didn't have the item for which they were looking. Rather than summarily sending them on their way, Elaine promised the couple that she would find the perfect piece for them, and requested their contact information.

She dutifully contacted our artists to see if they had anything that might work. I sent an email to all of the artists on our mailing list, with a description of what the clients were seeking.

Within twelve hours, our inboxes were overflowing with suggestions. The email we sent out was passed from artist to artist, and we soon found that the problem was not a dearth of viable options for the client, but rather a treasure trove of possibilities!

Elaine sifted through the images, and forwarded selections to the clients. We decided to send the images in small groupings, so as not to overwhelm them with all their newfound options.

Within the first grouping of six images, the couple saw something they liked. Elaine contacted the artist in Oklahoma, and asked her to send the piece out to us so we could show them the actual item for their inspection and approval.

When the piece arrived, we called the couple in to look at it. They loved the sculpture, but deemed the wood base to be inadequate. They asked us to find a replacement base, which should normally have proven easy enough to accomplish, but for one major challenge: their son's anniversary was now imminent, presenting us with a doozey of a deadline. We had a three day window in which to have the base constructed and delivered to the gallery.

After several hours of calling around, we found a base maker who made bases for one of our other sculptors. He was confident that he could create the base, have it shipped, and guarantee its arrival within the time allotted.

Our deadline was a Wednesday afternoon. The base arrived around 2:30, and I spent the next hour mounting the sculpture to the base, and attaching the name plate.

The couple made it into the gallery just before closing time, and were thrilled with the result. They completed the purchase, and provided us with their son's shipping address.

As we sat with them to finish the paperwork, the husband said, "You know, when we started our search, we visited half-a-dozen galleries and told them exactly what we were looking for. None of them had it, and they all tried to send us on a wild goose chase. When we told Elaine, she said she didn't have it, but that she would find it. We truly appreciate her efforts."

Kudos to Elaine. Not only did she make the sale, but she also built an incredible relationship with the couple. I won't be at all surprised if Elaine receives a holiday card at the end of the year. The next time they are looking for art, I feel certain they will begin their search at our gallery.

Of course, this scenario is more common for a gallery than for an independent artist – we have access to a variety of artists, and when we close a sale, we are able to collect a commission. To even the playing field, I would advise that an artist build a network of friends and contacts from the artists in his area, and from among the artists he meets at shows and festivals. I would counsel him to also study what is available in the local galleries.

Having thus made himself a valuable resource, the artist can put a call out to his network of connections to assist a client to find a desired artwork. The artist has every right to charge a finder's fee if he is able to facilitate a sale (15% is standard in the industry).

Offer to Clean Your Client's Artwork

One of the greatest challenges in building and maintaining strong relationships with collectors is the passage of time. Your customers will conceivably never stop liking you and admiring your work, but they might do something far worse: they might stop thinking about you at all.

Thankfully, there are ways to prevent this "out of sight, out of mind" circumstance. Marketing is as much about retaining former customers as it is about gaining new ones. So keep at the newsletters, the postcards, the open-studios – keep at whatever it takes to stay in front of the buyers. And don't ever allow the marketing regimen to grow stale: ramp it up a notch.

Want to do something that will put you both front and center in a collector's mind, and generate a boat-load of good will? Try this:

Pick up the phone today and call a past customer.

"Hi, this is _____. You purchased a piece of art from me called _____ about 18 months ago (or however long it's been). It's about time for the painting to be cleaned, and I want to set up a time that would be convenient for you, when I can stop by and do some basic preservation and maintenance. It will only take about fifteen minutes, and there's no charge. What does your schedule look like later this week?"

I recently started calling clients with this approach, and the response has been excellent. I'm not doing this as an overt pitch to make sales – that's really not what it is – I just want to provide excellent customer service, and encourage them to think about me the next time the urge to visit a gallery strikes.

The first customer I called was thrilled with the offer, but wanted to know how much it was going to cost him. When I insisted there would be no charge, he was shocked – I think he must have said "thank you" about a dozen times. While this obviously works best with local clients, when I travel, I look for opportunities to service out-of-town clients, as well.

Thus far, I've offered to clean bronze sculptures, which is a bit of a process – cleaning, waxing, and polishing – and also to clean paintings. Employing a dust rag and a can of compressed air (from Costco), while wearing white kid gloves, makes the process look impressively technical. When practicable, I take the painting off the wall to check the wire as well. Anything to please my valued friend. Anything to maintain an important relationship.

CHAPTER 12 | PRACTICE MAKES PERFECT

As mentioned in the introduction to this book, the sales process too often comes only as an after-thought for many artists, and even for some gallerists. There is a common perception that if one has quality art, he need merely get it in front of the right people and display it well, and the sales will naturally follow.

While some sales will certainly come as a matter of course, if one is not practicing salesmanship, he is sure to miss out on many sales. Salesmanship is a skill that has to be learned, cultivated, and most importantly, practiced. Like any skill, it will come more readily to some and will entail considerable work for others. Everyone, however, will benefit from practice.

Role Play

Practice your sales skills through role-playing. Ask a friend or family member (or another artist or gallerist – someone who will take the job seriously and provide honest feedback) to play the part of a customer. Suggest a variety of plausible scenarios which comprise a myriad of challenges to test your sales skills. This sort of exercise in improvisation is much akin to the exercise in which a pilot engages when he enters a flight simulator.

In the instance of the pilot, he is put into simulated flight situations to test, evaluate, and improve his flying skills. The various simulator paradigms are configured with true-to-life, in-flight conditions formulated to challenge the pilot's response, control, knowledge, instinct, judgment, technique, finesse, and acumen. The simulator is an excellent tool for providing a realistic reading relevant to a pilot's overall level of "aviation mastery", as well as to his measure of "innate giftedness" as an aviator. (Trained, experienced, and gifted: the definition of a *dream pilot*.)

To stay current and safe, the conscientious pilot gets as many hours in the flight simulator as money, time, and access will permit. He is, afterall, concerned about his own and his passengers' comfort and safety.

While the conscientious salesperson does not deal in issues of life-and-death, as does the pilot, she does have the desire (and the financial imperative!) to be proficient in the selling of art. She can test and measure her knowledge, skills, and gifts through the improvisation of "simulated sales scenarios". The paradigm for each scene should comprise unique personalities placed in difficult circumstances facing realistic obstacles. The plot possibilities and character descriptions are unlimited!

The artist or gallerist becomes dramatist, ready and willing to step into the character of salesperson in one scene, and collector in another. Learning to see a given situation from both sides of the transaction will work to her advantage in effectively strategizing a sale.

A plethora of interactive tools can be sharpened and seasoned through improvisational role-play: communication, cooperation, accommodation, adaptation, compromise, presentation, negotiation, resolution, and facilitation. Patience, perseverance, persistence, resilience, confidence, responsiveness, sincerity, civility, and creativity – all attributes of the superlative salesperson – ought to be portrayed through the persona of the artist/gallerist/vendor as she improvises the sales scene.

To make the activity an exceptional learning experience, record it; then watch, listen, and critique. Determine which aspects of the performance and delivery cry out for improvement. Invite others to offer objective opinions and considered recommendations. Tweak the tone of voice. Control the nervous ticks. Flash the friendly smile. Drop the offensive (or defensive) demeanor. Project more confidence. Show greater humility. Emanate optimism and good will. Talk less. Listen more.

No one likes to hear the unfamiliar sound of her own voice. No one enjoys watching himself play the fool on screen. In spite of the discomfort and awkwardness of hearing and seeing oneself improvise a role in a "make believe story", the lessons to be learned and the insights to be gained far outweigh any and all pain.

Soon after I opened the gallery, I did some self-recording of my interaction with clients, and asked my wife, Carrie, to critique my performance. I was doing some amazingly ridiculous things. First, my voice took an unnatural, high-pitched, singsong tone when I started talking with people. Why? Who knows. I didn't even realize it was happening – subconsciously, I might have been trying to appear pleasant; but it sounded ridiculous.

Even more embarrassing: I would hitch up my pants and make a show of tucking in my shirt as I stood up from the desk. Then, as I was standing in the gallery, inviting visitors to look around, I would re-tuck my shirt and hitch up my pants again, and yet again. One would think my clothes were falling off, and that I needed to buy smaller-waisted slacks. My clothes were fine; I just had an honest-to-goodness nervous tick. Though I had no idea I was doing it, Carrie laughed uproariously as she watched me play the clown.

"What on earth are you doing?" she choked.

"What?"

"Why are you constantly pulling up your pants?"

"What do you mean?" I asked. "I'm not. I don't know what you're talking about."

Of course, I was doing exactly what she said I was doing; right there on the video, as big as all life. I was horrified. Once Carrie pointed out this obnoxious habit, I began to catch myself doing it *all the time*. My pride was woefully wounded when she brought this behavior to my attention, but I would be re-tucking my shirt and hiking up my pants to this day, had she not!

(Keep in mind that this was soon after we opened our gallery in 2001, when I had already been in the business for almost eight years. Why on earth hadn't someone pointed out this buffoonish routine earlier? I guess I had never thought to ask.)

Ask! Better to have wounded pride for a day, than to act the fool for a lifetime.

Put Yourself in Selling Opportunities

Role-playing can provide valuable feedback, but there is nothing like live practice on the real world stage to give you experience. Interacting with customers gives you authentic experience that no amount of imagining and role-playing can simulate.

Look for opportunities to get your work out in front of buyers so that you can begin sharpening your skills. Displaying your work in weekend art festivals and shows is a great way to get front line experience in interacting with a large number of buyers. Opening your studio to participate in a local studio tour is another avenue to valuable interaction with potential buyers.

Think of your first forays into the market as practice. This will alleviate the pressure of feeling that you have to sell to be successful. Consider the event a success if you have the opportunity to talk to people about your work, and to practice your sales skills - even if you don't sell a single piece of art.

Break Down the Sales Process into Its Component Techniques, and Practice Them One at a Time

When practicing your salesmanship, don't look at the sales process as an overwhelming enterprise. Looking at it as a monolithic endeavor will make it seem too daunting to undertake. Rather, look at the road to sales success as being made up of small, manageable stepping stones, each stone representing a single skill. Work on mastering the process one stepping stone at a time, one skill at a time, as you progress along the cobblestone path toward your goal.

With your first venture into the market, you might focus solely on learning and using clients' names. Don't worry about accomplishing anything else. If you succeed in learning and using customers' names, consider yourself successful, and step onto a new stone to learn a new skill, during your next outing.

(If you don't initially master the skill, set a paradigm for an improvisation and reenact the experience until you feel sufficiently rehearsed to return to the real market, in real time, to learn, use, and remember real names.)

You will find, amazingly, that focusing on one skill at a time will lead to plenty of sales, even if you are not simultaneously practicing the other components of the process. The confidence you build by mastering the one skill will magically spill over to smooth every stone in the road that stretches before you. Over time, as you step onto the next stone, and the next, and onto the one after that, perfecting each subsequent skill as you go, you will become a master salesperson.

Remember, immediately prior to a showing, spend a few minutes reviewing the principle upon which you choose to focus during the event. I intentionally designed this book to be small enough to fit in a bag, from which it can be accessed for ready reference at any time deemed necessary or convenient.

Don't Skip Over the "Easy" Stuff

After reading this book, you might think that the most important chapters are those on closing the sale, resolving client concerns, and negotiating. I would suggest that the early chapters on building the initial relationship are every bit as vital to your ultimate success.

More importantly, no single step of the process works in total isolation. You cannot effectively resolve concerns and conflicts if you have not laid the groundwork based upon a relationship of trust. Building a relationship, but failing to ask for the close, might lead to friendship, but it will not lead to a sale.

I still maintain that you don't want to wait until you've mastered the whole process (you'd be waiting a long time), but nor do you want to ignore any vital element of procedure along the way.

Practice Checklist

I recommend that you work on mastering salesmanship skills by breaking the process down in the following order, and then practicing the skills one at a time:

1. Introductions (Chapter 2 | Introductions)

2. Learning Clients' Names (Chapter 3 | What's in a Name?)

3. Asking Questions (Chapter 4 | The Value of Questions)

4. Telling Stories About Yourself and Your Artwork (Chapter 5 | Create an Experience)

5. Helping Customers Visualize the Art in Their Space (Chapter 6 | Create a Vision)

6. Asking for the Close (Chapter 7 | Go for the Close)

7. Discovering and Resolving Concerns (Chapter 8 | Resolve Concerns)

8. Successfully Negotiating the Sale (Chapter 9 | Negotiate!)

9. Following Up (Chapter 10 | When all Else Fails, Follow Up)

CHAPTER 13 | OTHER CONSIDERATIONS

Prioritizing Customers When There Are Many of Them and Only One of You

We all run into situations in which we have more customers than we can deal with at a given moment. Sometimes clients don't conveniently stagger themselves, and instead, all come in at once. This is a common occurrence in a gallery setting, especially during an opening or an art walk.

While we work to give attention to as many customers as we possibly can, we also understand the folly of spreading ourselves too thin. Giving 1% of our attention to every person who walks through the door will likely result in 100 people who don't buy anything. It's better to focus in on one customer at a time, as though he were the only other person in the gallery.

In this scenario, I suggest that you give priority on a first-come, first-served basis. You may miss the opportunity to talk to other customers, but the clients you do work with will be appreciative of your attention, and therefore more likely to buy.

As detailed earlier in the book, you won't likely be intensely engaged with a potential buyer every moment of his visit to the gallery. When you step away to allow him space to look around, take the occasion to greet other visitors.

At a recent opening we held for an artist, I had a long-time client come into the gallery. Although we had a good crowd that evening, I spent over forty minutes with my client, and as a result, sold two pieces to him. Did I miss the opportunity to talk to other visitors? Indeed I did. Still, I have no doubt that the time I chose to spend with my established client was time well spent.

Though other visitors might not receive the attention you wish you could give them, the resulting impact will never be viewed as totally negative. After all, a full gallery or studio space sends the message to every visitor and every passer-by that you are successful, well-followed, and much-collected.

I often have buyers come back to the gallery in the days following a show. "We were here for the opening," they say, "but it was packed." They will then proceed to revisit the artwork, and I now have a chance to build a relationship and make a sale.

If you are occasionally faced with large crowds, it makes sense to bring in extra help, even if it's only temporary help. Have a spouse or friend help you at a studio opening. A gallery can bring in additional staff for shows. Make sure you have a brief training session prior to the opening of the show to make sure your help knows the basics – especially tasks like running the credit card machine, writing receipts, and recording sales. Offer a crash course in sales training, as well; suggest a few, simple pointers in professionalism.

Even though they cannot be expected to function as a fully trained and highly professional sales staff, your helpers can do much to ease the load of a heavy event. While you are occupied with managing the actual sales, hand off writing up the sales to a helper. Another assistant might be assigned to meet and greet, but told to refer specific questions to you for your informed responses. This is a great problem to have! Let the good times roll!

Words to Avoid

Over the years, I have found that certain words tend to throw a wet blanket on sales. There are words that sound scary in and of themselves, and words that perhaps at a subconscious level invoke doubt, and thus decrease sales. While you can't always avoid them, it's best to use other words instead whenever possible.

I find the words "price" and "cost" make things sound expensive – they pack a negative connotation. A *price* is something one "has to pay", and a *cost* is something that hurts one's pocketbook. As alternatives, try "value" or "worth". Doesn't "The value of this piece is $3,500", sound better than, "The price is $3,500", or "It costs $3,500"?

"Expense" is another word I avoid in reference to the value of a piece. It doesn't have a friendly ring.

"Buy" does not sound nearly as good as "acquire", and I am never going to let the word "sell" cross my lips when talking to a customer.

No one wants to "decide", or make a "decision". Decisions are always hard. Rather than ask someone if he has made a decision, I ask, "What would you like to do?"

Language is important. Keep the conversation positive. Avoid painting any negative mental pictures. Use words that are infused with light. Make a joyful sound!

Body Language

Another language you need to learn is the language your body speaks. Whether you intend it to or not, your body speaks volumes to your vistors.

Hands in pockets say, "I don't really take you seriously."

Folded arms say, "Don't approach me."

Scowling, frowning, furrowing of the brow, all send negative messages.

"I have matters of great importance on my mind."

"Could the day possibly get any worse?"

"This isn't where I want to be right now."

When I am listening to a customer, I hold my hands together in front of me, look into the customer's eyes, and lean in slightly to create a sense of intimacy. I want him to know he has my full attention.

A light touch on the arm is another way to make a connection. I would never want my customer to feel his space has been invaded, but a light touch to the arm, or a light brush to the shoulder to emphasize a point, will put him at ease. The touch should last no more than the blink of an eye, and should come only after establishing at least a modicum of rapport.

CHAPTER 14 | THE REALITIES

In sharing information on sales techniques, I will occasionally get a question to the effect:

"How many sales are you making in a day?" or "What percentage of walk-ins turns into sales?"

I always have mixed feelings about answering these sorts of questions because I fear the knowledge might be used as an excuse not to give 100% with every encounter.

On the other hand, I know that I would be doing you a disservice by not giving you the realities I have discovered. I don't want you to go out into the market with a false notion of what you are going to experience, only to have your expectations dashed.

You might think from reading this book that with the right skills and techniques, you can turn every person you meet into a buyer. Of course that is exactly how I would recommend you approach each prospective buyer; the reality, however, is that not everyone will be willing or able to buy from you. Only one "looker" in an afternoon of "lookers" will likely prove to be more than a disinterested browser.

If disappointment is not a risk for you, and you consider yourself an optimist who will never be dissuaded from your best efforts no matter what happens, you can stop reading right now. In fact, how about you save this chapter for when you have already been out into the real world and have some real experience. There's nothing like a little optimism to make good things happen. So no need to turn the page unless you've already started building sales experience.

Alright, you are either on this page because you're battle-worn and need some reassurance about the market, or the anticipation was killing you and you're cheating by reading ahead.

We might just as well start with a good dose of reality.

A number of years ago, I started a system to track how many visitors we were getting to the gallery, where the visitors had learned about us, and how many sales we were making. The system could not have been simpler. I created a spreadsheet that tracked visits for a week. Each day of the week had a series of boxes. We would fill in the designated boxes with an "x" for each visitor to the gallery. If the visitor had learned about our gallery through our marketing efforts, we would fill in another box with a designated code to signify the medium (a magazine ad, the internet, a post card, the radio, etc.). The final section comprised an area in which to record individual sales, together with their dollar amounts.

I never intended the tracking system to be permanent; I wanted to get a sense of our traffic patterns and the number of visitors we would have to see come through the gallery to have a sale. We ultimately recorded the data for a year or more. The results were interesting. I don't want you to take these numbers as scientific in any way. Furthermore, keep in mind that these numbers would be especially difficult to peg into disparate situations.

At the time, my gallery was located in an upscale retail plaza (we've since moved) that had consistent traffic. The center was in a great area in terms of demographics and income, and also attracted a good number of wealthy travelers. All positive aspects, of course. On the downside, most of the visitors to the center were not there looking specifically for art.

I give you this context so you can get a sense of how my gallery setting at the time would be different from that of a gallery in the heart of an arts district (as our gallery is now), or from the setting of an art show or festival, where people visit purposefully to look at art.

Enough dancing around – let's get down to some numbers.

On average, we found that on any given day, we would need to have between 90 – 120 people through the gallery before we could expect to make a sale. Pause a moment. Take a deep breath. Let those numbers sink in . . .

That means that we were putting forth our best effort to get to know, build relationships with, and attempt sales to about 100 customers before we were successfully closing *one sale*. If that number comes as a shock to you, perhaps you have not had a lot of sales experience.

To a certain extent, art sales are a numbers game. Some people who visit you are simply not going to be in a position to buy. They may not have the means or the interest. The timing may be wrong for them. Though you may have the most amazing work in the history of art, and put forth the best salesmanship the world has ever known, these folks are not going to buy.

On the other hand, you inevitably are going to encounter buyers who will see the art, and without hesitation, pull out their credit cards. They are primed and able to buy, even anxious to buy: all you have to do is process the sale, and handle the logistics.

For this class of buyers, your sales competence is largely irrelevant. These sales require little work, and are a lot of fun. Go ahead and credit these sales to your marketing and salesmanship prowess – it will do your confidence good.

Finally, you have those potential buyers in between the "never will" and "always will", who are interested and able, but will demand your full attention and assistance to help them acquire the work. In a real way, these are the buyers who make the difference. They are your bread and butter. There sadly aren't going to be enough of those who buy on their own accord to make you successful - and even if there were, you would want to be *more* successful yet!

Once we had an idea of how many visitors it took to make a single sale, we started working diligently to lower the ratio of visitors to buyers. It was great to have this new focus, and to see positive results.

Even at our best, however, we never broke the 80:1 barrier. Not at that location.

Let's think about the implications for a moment. If you are a gallery owner with a location that is only drawing 40-50 visitors per week, you will undoubtedly find it difficult to attain a level of sales sufficient to your need: the mathematics of the circumstance reflect a bleak outcome.

If you are an artist participating in an art festival, and have only a couple hundred people through your booth, it may not be enough to generate sales at a level that will offset your registration and space fees.

Ouch!

Numbers matter.

Again, though the numbers will vary depending upon the situation, the more eyeballs you have on the artwork, the more success you are going to reap in sales. Of course, it's also important to have the right people seeing the artwork – better to have one qualified and interested visitor than to have a thousand casual or uninterested browsers. You cannot expect to have much control on that front, though; not on a day-to-day, work-a-week basis.

However, our sales figures would increase significantly when we were having an opening for an artist, and specifically invited past collectors to attend the show. An article placed in local publications to feature the artist and her work, and to extend a welcome to the community for her show, raised all of our numbers.

A Brighter Reality

While a healthy dose of reality can sometimes taste like bad medicine, don't let yourself look at it that way. Knowledge is power, and knowing with certainty what challenges you face helps you confront and overcome them. Reach down deep for some of that "true grit" you've always known you have.

Let's look at some happier realities. We live in the greatest age ever for artists, for galleries, and for all those who dedicate their lives to art. There is a livelier market of art buyers out there than has ever before existed. Higher standards of living have allowed a broader group of people to participate in the art market at every level.

We also live in an age when getting your artwork out in front of collectors is simpler and more effective than it has ever been. Art galleries are spread over the face of the globe, and the internet has allowed us to get artwork in front of collectors even when they don't have physical access to a gallery or to a studio.

Though the economy can bounce around, a significant number of art buyers, from the avid collector to the novice lover, continues to look for opportunities to own quality works of art. Be you artist or gallerist, by taking a proactive approach to both getting your art in front of collectors, and to cultivating your skills to effectively assist people to acquire your art, you will build a rewarding, profitable career doing what you are most passionate about: creating and selling great art!

KEEP IN TOUCH!

Thank you for investing your time in reading this book, and for committing to improving your salesmanship. My goal in writing the book was to give you clear, understandable steps to immediately implement in your sales efforts.

I look forward to hearing from you as you employ these suggestions. Share your stories of triumph and defeat. Let me know if you have questions.

My direct email address is jason@xanadugallery.com. Though my inbox is always full, give me a few days and I will get back to you.

Interested in getting your art into galleries? Read my book "Starving" to Successful | The Fine Artist's Guide to Getting into Galleries and Selling More Art – available on our site at www.xanadugallery.com/book.

Interested in having me speak to your group? I speak to artist groups around the country on a variety of topics to assist members to achieve their professional goals. Contact me directly (jason@xanadugallery.com) for details.

The conversation continues on my blog at www.reddotblog.com. Visit the "How to Sell Art" tab for ongoing advice on how to be a better salesperson.